T0286875

Cambridge Elements ≡

Elements in Shakespeare Performance
edited by
W. B. Worthen
Barnard College

STAGING DISGUST

Rape, Shame, and Performance in Shakespeare and Middleton

Jennifer Panek
University of Ottawa

CAMBRIDGE
UNIVERSITY PRESS

CAMBRIDGE
UNIVERSITY PRESS

Shaftesbury Road, Cambridge CB2 8EA, United Kingdom

One Liberty Plaza, 20th Floor, New York, NY 10006, USA

477 Williamstown Road, Port Melbourne, VIC 3207, Australia

314–321, 3rd Floor, Plot 3, Splendor Forum, Jasola District Centre,
New Delhi – 110025, India

103 Penang Road, #05–06/07, Visioncrest Commercial, Singapore 238467

Cambridge University Press is part of Cambridge University Press & Assessment,
a department of the University of Cambridge.

We share the University's mission to contribute to society through the pursuit of
education, learning and research at the highest international levels of excellence.

www.cambridge.org
Information on this title: www.cambridge.org/9781009379823

DOI: 10.1017/9781009379816

First published 2024

A catalogue record for this publication is available from the British Library.

ISBN 978-1-009-37982-3 Paperback
ISSN 2516-0117 (online)
ISSN 2516-0109 (print)

Staging Disgust

Rape, Shame, and Performance in Shakespeare and Middleton

Elements in Shakespeare Performance

DOI: 10.1017/9781009379816
First published online: February 2024

Jennifer Panek
University of Ottawa

Author for correspondence: Jennifer Panek, jpanek@uottawa.ca

ABSTRACT: This Element turns to the stage to ask a deceptively simple question about gender and affect: what causes the shame of the early modern rape victim? Beneath honour codes and problematic assumptions about consent, the answer lies in an affect even more intractable than shame: disgust. Exploring both the textual "performance" of affect – how literary language works to evoke emotions – and the ways disgust can work in theatrical performance, this Element begins with Shakespeare's narrative poem *The Rape of Lucrece* as the classic paradigm of sexual pollution and shame, where disgust's irrational logic of contamination leaves the raped wife in a permanent state of uncleanness that spreads from body to soul. Staging disgust, however, offers alternatives to this depressing trajectory: Middleton's *Women Beware Women* and Shakespeare's *Titus Andronicus* perform disgust with a difference, deploying the audience's revulsion to challenge the assumption that a raped woman should "naturally" feel intolerable shame.

KEYWORDS: Shakespeare, Middleton, disgust, rape, shame

ISBNs: 9781009379823 (PB), 9781009379816 (OC)
ISSNs: 2516-0117 (online), 2516-0109 (print)

Contents

Introduction: Literature, Affect, and Performance

Part of my ongoing investigation into sexual shame in early modern English drama, this Element investigates what the performance of disgust can illuminate about the cultural and sexual dynamics that govern a subject for whom shame might seem to be the "natural" response: a married woman raped by a man who is not her husband. By the *performance* of disgust, I am invoking two separate but overlapping concepts. The first is the affective performance of literary texts, or how the skillful use of literary language evokes emotion in readers. The second is the deployment of affect in theatrical performance, or how the embodiment of a dramatic work on stage generates emotions in an audience – emotions that are integral to the meaning of the work itself. The first concept, the textual performance of affect, is central to my argument for how disgust and shame intersect in the nondramatic work with which this Element begins: Shakespeare's narrative poem *The Rape of Lucrece*. Offering the classic paradigm of a virtuous wife's rape requiring her suicide, the poem, I will argue, naturalizes and justifies Lucrece's unbearable shame by generating her for the reader, however briefly, as an object of disgust. I will then explore two plays that stage disgust in ways that put pressure on the logic by which an unwilling woman suffers shame for a man's crime.[1] The first is Middleton's *Women Beware Women*, which directs feelings of visceral disgust – both Bianca's and the audience's – toward the Duke as a strategy of affective justification for Bianca's *lack* of shame and her pragmatic choice to accept her rapist's offer of wealth, power, and protection rather than to end her life. I then turn to Shakespeare's *Titus Andronicus* – one of the period's most shockingly explicit performances of disgust in the context of rape – to demonstrate how it evokes the audience's disgust response toward Lavinia only to ultimately transfer it to her attackers in a move that rejects the Lucrece paradigm and its insistence that a rape victim should not, to use Titus's words, "survive her shame." This very selective examination of one

---

[1] This study makes no attempt to be a comprehensive survey of early modern rape narratives: my choice of texts is based primarily on the extent to which they feature the language of shame and disgust.

narrative poem and two plays is not intended as any kind of statement about the superior powers of drama to subvert oppressive assumptions about gender and sexuality; what it does reveal, though, is how far the power of bodies on stage can go beyond the affective performance of text to produce meaning through uncontrollable, visceral disgust.

The sense in which the language of literary texts performs affect for a reader – its artful evocation of specific emotional responses – is the focus of Alex Houen's introduction to a special issue of *Textual Practice* on "Affects, Texts, and Performativity." Houen begins with the performative or "illocutionary" speech act, J. L. Austin's terms for language that performs an action in its utterance, such as phrases like "I promise" or "I bequeath." Austin famously declared such acts "hollow or void if said by an actor in the stage, or if introduced in a poem, or spoken in soliloquy," but as Houen observes, this "exclusion of literature executes a socially instrumental view of language use partly by refusing to consider the affective and performative powers of language itself. For Austin, performativity is a matter of *people* doing things *with* language, not of language doing things to people." If, in Austin's terms, a "perlocutionary" speech act is one that "produce[s] certain consequential effects upon the feelings ... of the audience," the emotional response produced by literary writing is "intimately connected to how a text performs affects in an illocutionary fashion ... by reflexively structuring its emotional content in terms of what its formal devices are doing."[2] Citing poet and philosopher Denise Riley, Houen argues that language "exert[s] an *illocutionary* force of affect," performing the action of bringing emotions into being: "Language itself is indifferent to those who use it, and yet its 'very architecture' ... is inseparable from the feelings we form in relation to situations and others. Consequently, 'only a slight amplification of the notion of the performative [...] would let us think of language as a performer' in those situations, for language 'does not express feeling' so much as it 'does feeling.'"[3]

In Derek Attridge's compelling analysis of the same aesthetic/affective process, "performance" has a twofold meaning: not only does the text

---

[2] Austin, *How to Do Things with Words*, p. 101; Houen, "Introduction," 225.
[3] Houen, "Introduction," 216–217, 220.

perform emotions for the reader, in the illocutionary sense of calling them into being through language, but these emotions – including negative ones such as fear, grief, or horror – are experienced by the reader in a "performative" mode.[4] Starting from the premise that art, including literature, is a temporal "event ... that ... comes into existence, again and again, always differently, every time a reader, listener, or viewer experiences the arrangement of sounds or images as a work of art," Attridge argues that literary form, not merely a work's (fictional) affective content, is what generates a reader's emotional experience:

> [I]t's in response to the handling of form that the reader of a literary work brings it into being as literature. It's the writer's capacity to *shape* language in a temporal medium that endows it with pleasure-giving power. Any significant feature of language can be shaped this way, from the sounds of individual phonemes to the collocation of words to the flow of paragraphs and the structuring of chapters or whole novels. And it's through formed language that we're invited to participate in its emotion-arousing capacities; this means we feel the emotions, but always as performances of language's powers.... . The emotions experienced by the reader of a work of literature are real: of this there can surely be no doubt. That they are not identical with the emotions that would be felt as a result of direct exposure to the people and events portrayed is also, it seems to me, unquestionable. In arguing that the difference can be explained by regarding the reader's affective responses as performances of the emotions in question, I'm not suggesting that there is a conscious distancing at work: rather, it's a matter of the feelings being coloured by an awareness that they are being prompted by art – and this is a matter not primarily of fiction but of form.[5]

---

[4] Attridge, *Work of Literature*, p. 272. [5] Ibid., pp. 267, 279.

Literary form, then, can enable a reader's enjoyment of emotions that would be anything but pleasurable when experienced directly; nonetheless, these "performed" feelings – performed by the text, and experienced in a performative mode by the reader – are real and immediate. While Attridge attends primarily to *how* language, in the hands of a skillful author, can be shaped to evoke complex emotional responses, this study will be equally concerned with what these real and immediate feelings *do* – how disgust, in the case of the three works under consideration here, shapes the readers or audience member's perspective on the characters and events presented in a work of fiction.

Disgust, though, may well be an exception to Attrridge's hypothesis that emotions experienced in response to fiction are experienced in a "performative" mode. Carolyn Korsmeyer, drawing on the pioneering work of Aurel Kolnai, argues that disgust is a sufficiently "transparent" emotion to bypass the paradox of fiction – the puzzle of why we experience an emotional response to characters and events when we don't believe in their existence, and the question of whether these responses are phenomenologically the same as those evoked by "real life."[6] "[T]hat which is disgusting in nature remains disgusting in art," writes Korsmeyer. "Mimesis *transfers* but does not *transform* the disgusting image in art." The feeling, moreover, is identical to its "real life" equivalent:

> We are really disgusted even when we know the intentional object of disgust is a fiction. There is little gap between belief and emotion, because it is what is presented by the artwork itself that is the object of disgust. . . . Even with the full knowledge that the image is not of something really existing – say, a body opened for autopsy in a forensic TV drama – the disgust is still prompted by the image. No matter that we know it is not real; it is disgusting whether or not a real-life equivalent stands before one. . . . In short,

[6] For an overview of scholarship on the paradox of fiction, see Houen, "Introduction," 222–224; Korsmeyer, *Savoring Disgust*, pp. 53–56.

like the contributions of startle to fear, disgust is triggered immediately by elicitors that may be supplied equally well by reality or fiction.[7]

While early modern drama in performance does not typically engage with "the chief senses for disgust," taste and smell, it can and does avail itself of "vision and imaginative description" – and vision, in particular, "has a very large capacity to be disgusted."[8] Both *Women Beware Women* and *Titus Andronicus*, as I hope to demonstrate with reference to a range of modern productions, offer textual cues for the visual stimulation of disgust while simultaneously directing that disgust away from its conventional object in the contaminated body of the rape victim. When disgust is *staged* – evoked not by language alone but by the various embodied and sensory means available to actors and directors – its impact is arguably heightened. Numerous recent studies have explored the powerful transmission of affect in theatrical performance, on both the early modern and the modern stage; I am less interested here in *how* affect is transmitted in the theatre – the contagion of passions, the workings of mirror neurons, or the causes and effects of entrainment – than with the potential that transmission has to undermine certain conventional assumptions an audience may have about the scenario being played out on stage.[9] How might disgust work to

[7] Korsmeyer, *Savoring Disgust*, pp. 53, 56. Korsmeyer's comparison of disgust's instinctive recoil to fear's startle reflex – both "reflexive components" of their respective emotions – supports a concept of affect that recognizes the complex entanglement of autonomic, bodily reactions and cognition. My use of "affect / affective," "feeling," and "emotion" as relatively interchangeable terms throughout this Element reflects this view, which also follows Tribble, "Affective Contagion," and Attridge, *Work of Literature*, p. 261. As Tribble observes, Brian Massumi's influential theory of affect as purely pre-cognitive is less useful for understanding the affective practices of the theater than "contemporary models that place more stress upon the interplay between affect and cognition." See Tribble, "Affective Contagion," 197–198.

[8] Korsmeyer, *Savoring Disgust*, p. 57.

[9] Studies of the transmission of affect on the early modern stage include Roach, *Player's Passion*; Steggle, *Laughing and Weeping*; Hobgood, *Passionate Playgoing*;

reinforce – or to undermine – early modern cultural assumptions that rape creates in its victim a state of permanent and intolerable shame?

Disgust has been largely overlooked in feminist analyses of rape and shame in early modern literature and culture: the focus, instead, has been on the culture's peculiar logic concerning a woman's sexual consent, which produced shame by inculpating the victim in her own rape. In early modern legal contexts, the language used to talk about consensual sexual activity commonly depicted the female partner as "submitting" to the male or "suffering" him to have intercourse with her; an accusation of rape – of penetration without a woman's consent – thus meant she had been *forced* to submit. But when submission implies consent, rape is not forced penetration but forced *consent*.[10] A sensationalized version of this equation appears in the rape narratives that Jocelyn Catty finds to be "a standard feature" of Elizabethan prose romances, where rape becomes "yielding-rape" when a woman lacks the fortitude to choose the truly chaste, supposedly always-available alternative of death at her attacker's hands: "However resolutely she may have clung to the ideal of chastity, however she may have resisted, if verbal threats or physical violence induce her to *yield*, she is technically consenting."[11] "Consent" was similarly read into pregnancies that resulted from rape, on the assumption that female sexual pleasure was required for conception.[12] When rape is understood in these terms, the victim's shame appears as an unusually unfair version of shame for her own sin.

But the shame of rape, as I will argue, is also rooted in a set of basic and largely tacit assumptions about purity and pollution – assumptions which, to the best of my knowledge, have received little to no scholarly attention since Coppélia Kahn's 1976 article on *The Rape of Lucrece*.[13] Noting the poem's repetition of the word "stain" and its synonyms – "blot, spot, blur, blemish, attaint, scar, and pollution" – Kahn observes that

Mullaney, *Reformation of Emotions*; Tribble, "Affective Contagion." Affect in the modern theater is the focus of McConachie, *Engaging Audiences*; Hurley, *Theatre and Feeling*; Bernstein, "Towards the Integration."

[10] Walker, "Rereading Rape," 6. [11] Catty, *Writing Rape*, pp. 25, 32.

[12] Baines, "Effacing Rape," 80–81. [13] Kahn, "Rape in *Lucrece*," 49, 60.

though Lucrece uses moral terms such as sin and guilt, she actually condemns herself according to primitive, nonmoral standards of pollution and uncleanness, in which only the material circumstances of an act determine its goodness or evil.... . Marriage makes sex, and the woman as sexual object, clean; outside of marriage, sex is unclean. Once the pure, unsexual wife is brought into contact with sexuality outside marriage, though it be beyond her powers to avoid that contact, she is a polluted object. According to the anthropologist Mary Douglas, "Pollution rules are unequivocal, [and] do not depend on intention or on rights and duties. The only material question is whether a forbidden contact has taken place or not."[14]

Although part of Kahn's argument hinges on characterizing these pollution beliefs as pagan, at odds with the "Christian ethic" that Shakespeare weaves through the poem, it is hard to find much distance from them in literary representations of rape in early modern England.[15] Once the act of rape has occurred, the victim's shame is thoroughly entangled with the most material, most physical aspects of this "stain," this "pollution," this "uncleanness."

Before going further, I should clarify two things about "disgust" as a concept and as a term. First, this study does not attempt to separate out what is usually termed "moral disgust" from "physical disgust," the aversive affect that evolved as protection from pathogens and parasites, which psychologists have labeled "core disgust."[16] The language used to express abhorrence of moral transgressions has long overlapped with that used to reject filth: we can declare ourselves "disgusted" by a lying politician or by

---

[14] Ibid., 47, 49, 60.

[15] See, for instance, Sanchez, *Erotic Subjects*, p. 87; Bamford, *Sexual Violence*, p. 122. As Bamford concludes, "the question that determines [the raped woman's] fate is not moral but material, not 'is she *morally* chaste?' but 'is she – or can she remain – *vaginally* chaste'?" Kahn's later work on *Lucrece* revises some of her earlier claims: see Kahn, *Roman Shakespeare*, p. 42.

[16] On core disgust, see Kelly, *Yuck!*, pp. 17–21.

an unflushed toilet, just as Edward Reynolds, writing c. 1640, could switch between the physical and moral valences of "loathe" to compare wine in a revoltingly dirty cup to virtuous speeches in the mouth of a depraved speaker:

> For as a man receiveth the selfe same Wine with pleasure in
> a pure and cleane Vessell, which he loaths to put unto his
> mouth, from one that is foule and soiled: so the selfe same
> Speech adorned with the Piety of one man, and disgraced
> with the Pravity of another, will be very apt accordingly to
> be received, either with delight or loathing.[17]

The difficulty with talking about "moral disgust," however, is that there is no consensus, even among modern psychologists and theorists of affect, as to precisely what it *is*. Different theorists argue for different definitions: "moral disgust," in one view, is purely metaphorical, and "disgust" at liars and hypocrites is like "lust" for designer shoes or a "thirst" for knowledge; in another, it is an affect produced by a cluster of specific vices, including hypocrisy, betrayal, fawning, and cruelty. Rachel Herz considers "moral disgust" to be the feeling aroused by moral violations containing a component of bodily disgust, such as prohibited sexual acts or particularly grisly murders; Daniel Kelly theorizes it to be the result of an evolutionary process in which core disgust, as humans grew more social, became entangled with and co-opted by cognitive systems involved in social interactions so that the affect that originally protected us from eating tainted food eventually attached itself to, say, copulating with our siblings.[18] To complicate the matter further, studies have shown that inducing physical disgust increases moral severity – for instance, subjects obliged to sit in disgustingly dirty workspaces and rate moral offenses do so more harshly than their counter-parts in clean workspaces – and that people (e.g., religious conservatives)

---

[17] Reynoldes, *Treatise of the Passions*, p. 509.

[18] In order, these definitions are from Rozin, Haidt, and McCauley, "Disgust," 821–822; Miller, *Anatomy*, pp. 185–186; Herz, *That's Disgusting*, pp. 188–193; and Kelly, *Yuck!*, pp. 116–136.

who place moral significance on a wide array of acts and issues are notably more sensitive to physical disgust than people who do not.[19] When does moral condemnation become moral disgust? What is the relationship between moral disgust and physical disgust? When is moral disgust really just physical disgust mistaken for morality?[20] There is little agreement on the answers to such questions. With its disputed relationship to moral condemnation on one side and to physical disgust on the other, the concept of "moral disgust" remains vague and slippery. Therefore, while links between disgust and moral condemnation are everywhere in texts dealing with rape, I will simply analyze them in their individual contexts without attempting to define "moral disgust" or to treat it as a separate category of affect from the physical disgust – the nausea of surfeit, the recoiling from filth, the anxiety over contamination – that will be the focus of this study. Nor, by the same token, will I be considering as "disgust" instances of moral condemnation that bear no immediate relation to bodily recoil. The word "disgust," in what follows, will always have a strong physical valence.

Second, it's important to point out that the word "disgust" itself appears in none of the primary texts that form the core of this study, as they date from a period in which it was only just beginning to acquire its modern meaning. If a precise line between moral and physical disgust is hard to draw, distinctions between modern and early modern experiences of disgust are at least equally so. For an affect that functions as a demarcator of boundaries – pure versus impure, familiar versus foreign, civilized versus uncivilized – and whose cultural specificity goes without saying (one diner's *Époisses* is another's *natto* is another's *balut*), disgust is oddly resistant to historicization's usual methods of estrangement. Benedict Robinson's enlightening history of how the word "disgust" entered the English language over the course of the seventeenth century shows its evolution from something akin to "dislike" with overtones of conflict – gambling, for

---

[19] Herz, *That's Disgusting*, pp. 187–188, 191.

[20] Ibid., p. 199. Herz discusses "moral dumbfounding": "the irresistible feeling to castigate a behavior as wrong simply because it crosses a taboo and disgust threshold."

instance, could lead to "disgusts" between players – to its modern meaning of "sensory revulsion."[21] Robinson also makes a persuasive argument for how the realm of affective experience circumscribed by the Latinate "disgust" came to be carved out of the larger sphere defined by the Anglo-Saxon "loathing": loathing, as he describes it, is "intense and unremitting," replete with ethical and religious connotations, and "harbors little of the ambivalence of disgust and few of its shades of variation," while "disgust" finds its territory in "the terrain . . . of aesthetics or dietetics," does not insist on the "ethical intelligibility" of bodily experience, and does not unambiguously exclude pleasure or desire. As Robinson notes at the outset, though, the seventeenth-century innovation of "disgust" does not mean that we are dealing with a new feeling: "Disgust has been described as one of the basic emotions found in all cultures, a drive coded into us by evolution."[22] On one hand, then, we would seem to have "disgust" taking on the recognizable semblance of the modern affect in the years roughly coterminous with the texts to be examined here – Robinson's central exemplar of innovations in "disgust" is Ben Jonson's epigram "On the Famous Voyage," written c. 1610 – while on the other, "loathing" still encompassed some of the territory to be ceded to disgust. That the wider sphere of "loathing" was freighted with ethical significance does not seem to have precluded the word's use for purely physical revulsion, let alone precluded the existence of such revulsion. Reynolds' wine drinker, from the example quoted earlier, who "loaths" to put a "foule and soiled" cup to his lips, is arguably in the realm of ethically neutral disgust, and the patient who lacks appetite due to a bad spleen, whose "Stomacke consequently suffreth cruditie, loathing of meate, and is much infested wyth breakinge of sower wynde upwarde," likely attaches no ethical significance to the food he rejects.[23] In their introduction to *Disgust in Early Modern English Literature*, Natalie K. Eschenbaum and Barbara Correll tread a careful line between resisting disgust's seductive pull toward transhistorical readings and recognizing that for this particular affect, the rich body of modern scholarship on disgust can prove illuminating for the study of early modern texts. "It is crucial to look

---

[21] Robinson, "Disgust c. 1600," 557. [22] Ibid., 569, 554–555, 553.

[23] Lemnius, *Touchstone*, p. 142.

back," they warn, ". . . to the practices and philosophies that informed early modern writers' expressions or representations of aversion" – but even as they and their contributors do so, they draw on the work of modern cultural scholars, psychologists, philosophers, and affect theorists, practicing what the editors describe as "close cultural and literary reading in which contemporary affect theory, among other conceptual and interdisciplinary tools, might prove to be helpful, if not determining."[24] My approach here is similar, paying close attention to the early modern language and contexts of disgust as it intersects with shame in the rape narratives under examination, while applying, when useful, the interpretive tools offered by the wealth of modern scholarship on this particular affect. Whether due to its universal evolutionary function, its collapsing of representation and reality, or some other reason, disgust repays such an approach, stretching out its sticky hand across the centuries.

Early Modern Sexual Pollution

"Such abhorred pollution" (3.1.183) is Isabella's term in *Measure for Measure* for the effect that nonmarital intercourse would have on her chaste body – a word rooted in physical filth, from the Latin "lutum" (mud) (*OED* "pollute," v.).[25] Kahn's observation, quoted earlier, that "marriage makes sex, and the woman as sexual object, clean; outside of marriage, sex is unclean" applies, of course, to all nonmarital sex, not just adultery, and her specifications of both "*woman*" and "sexual *object*" are key.[26] For a man, depending on the circumstances, nonmarital sex can be enervating and effeminating, it can be sinful, it can be damaging to his reputation, but unless his sexual encounters literally contaminate him – that is, they infect him with the "foul disease" – it is not polluting in anything more than the moral, metaphorical sense: it does not make him *dirty*.[27] But if dirt, in Mary Douglas's famous phrase, is "matter out of

---

[24] Eschenbaum and Correll, "Introduction," 2, 5.
[25] All Shakespeare quotations are from *The Norton Shakespeare* unless otherwise stated.
[26] Kahn, "Rape in *Lucrece*," 60.
[27] On syphilis as "the foul disease," see Siena, "Clean and Foul," 261–284.

place," then semen ejaculated into anything other than the body of the ejaculator's wife becomes dirt, and the object that receives it – the "receptacle / Of luxury and dishonour" (5.1.99–100), to borrow an epithet that a man uses for his pregnant unwed sister in Middleton's *The Nice Valour* – is inescapably soiled.[28] "Thou shalt not lye with thy neighbour's wife," warns Thomas Becon in *The Governaunce of Vertue*, "to defile her with sede": that Becon here seems to be misremembering the wording of Leviticus 18:20, "Thou shalt not give thyself to thy neighbour's wife in carnall copulation, to be defiled with her," speaks to the assumption that male sexual fluids "defile" – another word with its roots in disgusting muck, this time of rot, pus, and stench – the woman in a quite literal way, even as the man shares the sin.[29] We need not accept all of William Ian Miller's rather extraordinary exposition on what he calls the "most polluting of male substances" to note that semen has the "primary disgust features" of being "slimy, sticky, and viscous" and that it "makes the vagina the site of rank fecundity and generation that assimilates it to the constellation of images that makes teeming, moist, swampy ooze a source of disgust."[30] Miller also takes us back to an early modern context when he quotes Thomas Nashe's fulminations against whores in *Christs Teares Over Jerusalem* (1593), where the semen that is deposited into the professional prostitute is figuratively lowered, on a scale of unequivocally disgusting bodily products, to the level of feces: "What are you but sincks

---

[28] Douglas, *Purity and Danger*, p. 36. Douglas is quoted in Kahn, "Rape in *Lucrece*," 60. All Middleton quotations are from *Thomas Middleton: The Collected Works* unless otherwise stated.

[29] Becon, *Governaunce*, p. 87. Becon's marginal note cites Exodus 10, but that chapter contains no such verse. According to the *OED*, "defile" (v.1) is from "defoul," a word linked by the fourteenth century to "foul," whose Greek, Latin, and Sanskrit roots have to do with stink, rot, and "prurulent matter."

[30] Miller, *Anatomy*, pp. 103–104. His insistence that "semen has the extraordinary power conferred on it by patriarchy to feminize whatever it comes into contact with," and that it is "of all sex-linked disgust substances, the most revolting to *men*" is clearly based in assumptions that are both heteronormative and markedly modern; early modern perceptions of whether semen disgusts, let alone feminizes, are strongly context-dependent.

and privies to swallow in men's filth?'"; Hippolito levels a similar accusation at the prostitute Bellafront in Middleton and Dekker's *The Honest Whore, Part I*: "For your body, / It's like the common shore, that still receives / All the town's filth. The sin of many men is within you" (6.376–379).[31] It was, as Gail Kern Paster has shown, "wholly conventional" to trope the prostitute as a privy: "the body of the whore and the privy alike serve as receptacles for bodily emissions, for the products of 'like evacuations.' Yet, as an 'excremental vessel,' the whore's body functions not only in the way of the degraded body generally, as mere container of its own excrement, but more particularly as the doubly-debased receptacle of *public* excrement."[32] We might note Sarah Toulalan's caution that the early modern economy of bodily fluids, in which "everything was interrelated," means that early modern equations of the sexual with the scatological do not necessarily carry their modern "overtones of dirt and disgust," as excretion and purgation frequently had positive associations with health.[33] While one can think, however, of gentler versions of the semen / feces equation, such as Freevill's quip, in Marston's *The Dutch Courtesan*, that a whore might euphemistically be called a "suppository" (1.2.102) – the former, presumably, makes you ejaculate, just as the latter purges your bowels, with the destination of your products left decorously unspecified – tropes that figure the whore's body as a privy or sewer are clearly *meant* to disgust, such as when Isabella's horror of "pollution" finds its perverse match in her would-be defiler's equally horrified urge to pollute:

> Having waste ground enough
> Shall we desire to raze the sanctuary,
> And pitch our evils there? O fie, fie, fie!
> What dost thou, or what art thou, Angelo?
> Dost thou desire her foully for those things
> That make her good? (2.2.174–179)

---

[31] Nashe is quoted in Miller, *Anatomy*, p. 104.
[32] Paster, *Body Embarrassed*, pp. 154–155. [33] Toulalan, *Imagining Sex*, p. 199.

For Angelo to satisfy his "foul" desires within the "sanctuary" of Isabella's body would be to turn it, and her, into a latrine – an image he might recall when, shortly afterward, he asks if she would "give up her body to... sweet uncleanness" (2.4.53); the adjective "sweet," juxtaposed with "unclean," hovers between a figurative "pleasurable" and a more literal, paradoxical "fragrant."[34] "Fie" could express disgust as well as scorn or condemnation, and could in fact function in early modern stage dialogue as a signal for gagging or spitting.[35] While we might be inclined to imagine the fastidious Angelo's series of "fies" as a self-administered scolding that begins the address to himself that follows, reading the "fies" instead as a conclusion to the previous statement raises the possibility in performance of an Angelo disgusted to the point of gagging at the thought of the pure Isabella befouled with his seminal/fecal filth.

Somewhat less conventional, and thus perhaps even more revealing of early modern revulsion toward the sexually polluted woman, are images that resonate with what modern theorists posit as a prototypical object of disgust: decay, and its accompanying, uncanny fertility. The specific disgust value of rot was first articulated by Kolnai in his 1927 essay "Der Ekel" ("Disgust"):

> The mark of a disgusting object is found quite specifically in the process of putrescence, and in its carrier. . . . In general we repeat once more that something dead is never disgusting in its *mere non-functioning* . . . . Rather, substantial decomposition is necessary, which must at least seem to put itself forward as a continuing process, almost as if it were after all just another manifestation of life. Already here we encounter the relation of disgust to what is positively vital, to what is animated. And indeed there is undoubtedly associated with the extinction of life in putrefaction a certain – quite remarkable – augmentation of life: a heightened announcement of the fact

---

34 Compare *OED* "sweet" adj. 2a and 5.

35 Robinson, "Disgust c. 1600," 559; compare Lear's "Fie, fie, fie! pah! pah!" (4.6.126).

that life *is there*. Evidence of this is provided by the reinforced smell that accompanies putrefaction, the often glaring change of colors, the putrefied "sheen," the whole phenomenon of turbulence characteristic of putrefaction.[36]

Bodily wastes, as "decomposed organic matter [that] indicates existence, or past existence, of life"; bodily secretions like mucus and semen, which offer "'an indecent surplus of life' ... that, true to nature, points once more to death and to putrefaction"; and vermin, with "their pullulating squirming; their cohesion into a homogenous teeming mass; their evocation – partly apparent, partly real – of decomposition and decay," all participate in this central category.[37] Echoing Kolnai, Miller terms the core disgust object "life soup":

> Images of decay imperceptibly slide into images of fertility and out again. Death thus horrifies and disgusts not just because it smells revoltingly bad, but because it is not an end to the process of living but part of a cycle of eternal recurrence. The having lived and the living unite to make up the organic world of generative rot – rank, smelling, and upsetting to the touch.[38]

When in *Much Ado About Nothing*, Claudio returns the putatively unchaste Hero to her father as "a rotten orange," Shakespeare provides not merely an abstract symbol for a supposed virgin who is "but the sign and semblance of her honour" (4.1.30–31) – that is, deceptively attractive without and worthless within – but an image of quite literally palpable disgust: anyone who has unwittingly grasped a rotten orange from among a pile of good ones knows the shudder of having your fingers sink softly into something

---

[36] Kolnai, *Disgust*, p. 53. [37] Ibid., pp. 54–57.

[38] Miller, *Anatomy*, p. 40; see also pp. 41–43 for several early modern examples of disgust with "generative rot." Miller does not cite Kolnai; for an account of the overlap between the two theorists, see Korsmeyer and Smith's introduction to Kolnai, *Disgust*, pp. 3, 16–18.

you expect to be firm. Miller's list of the dichotomies that structure disgust includes "firm vs. squishy"; Kolnai points out that rotten meat and rotten fruit share the "optical-tactile-olfactory formation" that triggers disgust, with "a similarity of coloration, not to speak of other common features such as softening."[39] The intact, barely ripe, and aesthetically pleasing body of the virgin girl that Claudio had anticipated grasping in marriage has proven spoiled, "yielding," in both the moral and the tactile senses of the word, and dismayingly similar to the body of the old woman – "an obscene, decaying corpse in her own lifetime" – with its "excessive softness" and "loathsome discharges," that, according to Winfried Menninghaus, is disgust personified.[40] The move from rotten fruit to the more explicitly repulsive rotten meat comes only a few lines later, when Leonato, convinced of his daughter's sexual pollution, laments that the sea itself contains "salt too little which may season give / To her foul tainted flesh" (4.1.141–142).

A more elaborate image of the polluted wife as a site of fertile decay appears in *Othello*:

> But there where I have garnered up my heart,
> Where either I must live or bear no life,
> The fountain from which my current runs
> Or else dries up – to be discarded thence,
> Or keep it as a cistern for foul toads
> To knot and gender in. (4.2.59–64)

In Othello's tortured metaphor, both the garner, a dry storehouse for grain, and the "fountain" or spring, a source of clean, running water, are transformed into the cistern, thus wetting the garner, rotting the grain, and rendering the fountain stagnant, enclosed, and prone to slime. There are enough toads in there to "knot" ("one vs. many" is another of Miller's structuring dichotomies of disgust) and they are producing, through whatever unsightly mating toads engage in, yet more toads: toads and their

---

[39] Miller, *Anatomy*, p. 38; Kolnai, *Disgust*, p. 53.
[40] Menninghaus, *Disgust*, pp. 7–8.

copulation, as detailed in Karl P. Wentersdorf's essay on "sex nausea" in *Hamlet*, vividly combined repulsiveness and sexual depravity in the early modern imagination.[41] If we read the fountain as the Norton editors do – "the language here imagines Desdemona as the source of Othello's future offspring" – then the passage takes us from the unspecified "there" of Desdemona, to her womb, as "the fountain from which [Othello's] current runs," to that "cistern" where the "knotting" and "gendering" take place. The imaginary unfaithful Desdemona becomes a *mise-en-abyme* of disgust, copulating slimily with Cassio in a space that represents her own dank and obscenely capacious vagina.[42] Othello's follow-up to this image – his bitter gibe that Desdemona is as honest "as summer flies are in the shambles / That quicken even with blowing" (4.2.68–69) – is even more graphically vile. It makes most sense, I think, if we read not "flies" but "shambles," a synecdoche for the meat butchered within them, as the subject of "quicken," or, conversely, if we read the flies as "quickening" *something else*. In either case, the image evokes not just the speedy life cycle of flies and their eggs, but tainted, flyblown meat on a hot summer's day, "quick" with writhing maggots. As it would be Desdemona herself who would "quicken" with the product of her adultery, she would seem to begin as the flies but end as the meat, infested with offspring as a result of being "blown" by another man's fertile seed.

Maggots can spread; a rotten orange taints the oranges around it; if the cistern is for drinking water, fishing out the toads is hardly enough to make anyone want to drink the water left inside. One of the most striking characteristics of the disgusting is its powerful ability to contaminate:

> There may be in the cup
> A spider steeped, and one may drink, depart,
> And yet partake no venom, for his knowledge

---

[41] Miller, *Anatomy*, p. 38; Wentersdorf, "Animal Sybolism," 369–371.

[42] Reading "there" (l. 59) and "it" (l. 63) as referring to Desdemona follows Pechter, *Othello*, p. 89, who adds that the "it" becomes "grotesquely specific" [i.e., as a genital reference] with the passage's "final image of the angel's rosy lips."

> Is not infected; but if one present
> Th'abhorred ingredient to his eye, make known
> How he hath drunk, he cracks his gorge, his sides,
> With violent hefts. I have drunk, and seen the spider. (*The
> Winter's Tale* 2.1.41–47)

Leontes' famous lines are ostensibly not about how he feels about
Hermione: rather, he is congratulating himself on his insight into the
faithlessness of Camillo, who has just been reported to have fled with
Polixenes. The men's flight, however, confirms his suspicions of
Hermione's adultery, and, significantly, Leontes' very next move takes
him mentally from the spider-beverage to other liquids, when he seques-
ters Mamillius from his mother as a font of contamination: "I am glad you
did not nurse him . . . yet you / Have too much blood in him" (2.1.57–59).
The supposedly adulterous Hermione is contaminating because she herself is contaminated: Leontes' references to blood and to breast milk,
a blood-derived substance, leave unspoken the third and most disgusting
blood-concoction contained in Hermione, namely Polixenes' semen.[43]
The "spider in the cup" metaphor, with its vivid evocation of nauseated
retching, is thus a sexually inflected version of the most elemental food-
disgust situation, one mentioned in René Descartes *The Passions of the
Soul*: "when one unexpectedly comes upon something very foul in food he
is eating with relish, the surprise of this encounter can so change the
disposition of the brain that he will no longer be able to see any such food
afterwards without abhorrence, whereas previously he used to eat it with
pleasure."[44] Paul Rozin and April E. Fallon's extensive study of this
particular aspect of disgust lays out the scientific underpinnings of
Descartes' observation, demonstrating how "revulsion at the prospect of
(oral) incorporation of an offensive object" extends far beyond any
material threat posed by that object. Not only are "the offensive

---

[43] On the fungibility of fluids in the Galenic body, see Paster, *Body
Embarrassed*, p. 9.

[44] Descartes is quoted and briefly discussed in Robinson, "Disgust
c. 1600," 554.

objects . . . contaminants" so that "if they even briefly contact an accep-
table food, they tend to render that food unacceptable," but the "contact"
between contaminant and food can be wholly psychological, as demonstrated by an experiment in which subjects rejected juice that had held
a sterilized cockroach, and then went on to reject perfectly clean juice, in
a new glass, that happened to be of the same *kind* as the juice in which they
had previously seen the cockroach.[45] Leontes' claim to a related
experience – "I have drunk, and seen the spider" – offers a fascinating
example of disgust due to psychological contamination. According to the
Arden edition's footnote to the "spider" passage, the idea that the spider-
contaminated drink is harmless if the drinker does not see the spider, but
poisonous if he does, is Leontes' own peculiar variation on popular beliefs
about spiders and their venom. A search for "spider NEAR cup" in *Early
English Books Online* corroborates this claim, as it turns up two separate
versions of a parable on Catholic error in which a guest asks his host's
permission to remove a spider from a proffered cup of wine before he
drinks it: the guest is clearly of the belief that ingesting the spider would
be dangerous, but consuming the remaining wine would not be.[46] Leontes
would seem to be claiming that his is less a disgust reaction than what
Rozin and Fallon term a "danger" rejection, where the refusal of a food,
such as poisonous mushrooms, is based on anticipated harmful effects: the
heaving and cracking of the gorge upon seeing the spider thus becomes, in
Leontes' version, at least much the drinker's attempt to vomit up the
poisonous beverage before it can harm him as the involuntary effect of
revulsion.[47] An audience member, however, who is familiar with the
traditional version of the belief – spiders are poisonous, but wine that
has previously held a spider is not – can see how Leontes is taking a basic
disgust reaction – "one unexpectedly comes upon something very foul in
food he is eating with relish" – and inventing around it a tale of prudent
avoidance of danger. The spider passage therefore mirrors his insistence
throughout the first half of the play that he is working with certainties

[45] Rozin and Fallon, "Perspective on Disgust," 23–24, 30, 37.
[46] Vertue, *Plea*, pp. 42–43; Hall, "Noah's Dove," 516–517.
[47] Rozin and Fallon, "Perspective on Disgust," 24.

based in fact (Camillo and Polixenes' flight is proof positive of guilt, he insists, just as a visible spider makes wine poisonous), not irrational impulses based in feeling (jealousy, as he fails to realize, should not be taken as evidence that there is something to be jealous about; everyone knows that once the spider has been removed, the wine should rationally be recognized as harmless, despite the impulse to find it disgusting). The liquid in the cup, like the body of the wife, suddenly transformed from enjoyable to revolting by the presence of a foreign substance, further extends its contaminating reach to the person who experiences disgust through contact with it: "The mere sensation of [disgust] also involves an admission that we did not escape contamination. The experience of disgust, in other words, does not itself purify us in the way the experience of anger or indignation can. Disgust signals the need to undertake further labors of purification."[48] That Leontes wants Hermione and the product of her supposed adultery not just put to death but specifically "given to the fire" (2.3.8; see also 2.3.96 and 2.3.134) – the most powerfully purificatory element of the four – suggests the extent of his need to de-contaminate himself.

The disgusting object's impressive powers of contamination take us back to the subject of rape. The sexual pollution and hence the disgust-ingness of Hermione, Hero, Desdemona, or Isabella exist entirely in the minds of the men describing them in such terms; while this language might briefly evoke disgust, generating an image of the women as they are described, the fiction is strongly invested in representing the men as wrong and the women as "actually" pure. When disgust comes into play in a rape scenario, however, the act culturally assumed to constitute bodily pollution *has* occurred, and the physical, visceral nature of disgust is utterly unconcerned with the volition of the contaminated object or the conditions under which contamination takes place. Disgust, as Sara Ahmed aptly puts it, treats its object "as if the object contained the 'truth' of our own response to it": "I feel sick, you have sickened me, you are sickening."[49] And to "be" disgusting – to have the disgust of others directed at oneself – is a potent cause for shame.

[48] Miller, *Anatomy*, p. 204. [49] Ahmed, *Cultural Politics of Emotion*, p. 85.

The Rape of Lucrece

To illustrate how disgust can provide an underlying affective justification for the logically unjustified shame of an innocent victim, I want to turn to Shakespeare's narrative poem, *The Rape of Lucrece*. The question of why a rape victim – if she were indeed innocent – should have felt intolerable shame for a crime perpetrated against her was carefully considered by St. Augustine, who reached a notoriously problematic conclusion. Rape, he decided, "engender[s] a sense of shame because it may be believed that an act, which perhaps could not have taken place without some physical pleasure, was accompanied also by a consent of the mind." As Virginia Burrus observes, Augustine's suggestion that Lucrece's suicide could have been self-punishment for being "so enticed by her own desire that she consented to the act," leads into a downward spiral of uncertainty:

> Only Lucretia could know whether [her intentions] are pure, and Augustine can only imagine that they might not be. Perhaps even Lucretia couldn't know: in the face of such relentless scrutiny of the heart's secrets, the line between rape and seduction may become nearly impossible to detect. How could she be absolutely sure that no part of her will, however small, submitted to the mastery of lust (his, hers), however briefly? Even as he revoices the comforting assurances of Lucretia's father and husband – 'without intention there could never be guilt' – Augustine virtually eradicates the possibility of affirming innocence by placing intention beyond the reach of certainty while also requiring that it always be pure.[50]

Feminist critics of Shakespeare's *The Rape of Lucrece*, however, tend to agree that the poem presents Lucrece's suicide as a virtuous act, and not as self-punishment for sin. While the poem does not ignore the complexities

[50] Burrus, *Saving Shame*, pp. 127–128; Augustine is quoted in Burrus. The same passage is also discussed in Baines, "Effacing Rape," 80–81.

and even ironies of its efforts to reconcile the Christian sin of suicide to a Roman virtue, the reader is not invited to judge Shakespeare's Lucrece by Augustinian standards as guilty of the dual sins of pride and self-murder.[51] And if one is to recognize Lucrece's suicide as a virtuous or at least well-intentioned act, then her sense of shame – its rightness and its inevitability – must be accepted on the terms that she and the narrator establish.

Shakespeare thus sets himself the task of writing a Lucrece who is both innocent of any sinful intent, *and* filled with a shame so powerful and so permanent that life in that shamed state would be unbearable. In her study of how Shakespeare deploys rhetorical figures in *The Rape of Lucrece* to "manipulate. . .our moral and emotional responses to his personages," Heather Dubrow draws attention to the poem's use of syneciosis: "a statement that uncovers similarities in two seemingly dissimilar things." A description of Tarquin, for instance, as "A captive victor that hath lost in gain" (730), includes not only the oxymoron (itself a form of syneciosis) of "captive victor" but the recognition that "losing can be gaining and gaining losing." Holding its two dissimilar elements in tension without opposing them to each other, the figure effectively evokes "ambiguous intermediate states, such as the sensation of being both dead and alive or the dilemma of

---

[51] Kahn, "Rape in *Lucrece*," 65, maintains that Shakespeare's Christian perspective holds Lucrece to be pure and her suicide "tragically ironic." The "Christian perspective" thesis is challenged by Bromley, "Lucrece's Re-Creation," 200–201, who summarizes earlier claims that Shakespeare condemns Lucrece for overvaluing her reputation, and argues that the poem presents Tarquin's corruption of Lucrece as "a simple fact, accepted by Lucrece and her society and by Shakespeare and his society." See also Williams, "Silence," 95 and Donaldson, *Rapes of Lucretia*, p. 49: both note contradictions in Shakespeare's treatment of Lucrece, caused by the simultaneous operation of "shame" and "guilt" values in early modern England. Feminist critics after Bromley differ on the extent to which Lucrece upholds or challenges patriarchal assumptions, but generally agree that Lucrece's own perspective on her violation is also the poem's: see, for instance, Maus, "Tropes"; Newman, "Mild Women"; Belsey, "Tarquin Dispossessed"; Daileader, "Writing Rape." On the morality of Lucrece's suicide as a subject of debate for early modern readers, see Roberts, *Reading Shakespeare's Poems*, pp.102–113.

being at once chaste and unchaste."[52] Dubrow does not focus specifically on Lucrece's shame, and, in what follows, I will be more concerned with the poem's use of imagery to evoke disgust than with specific rhetorical figures, but those "ambiguous intermediate states" are very much to the point. The reader's sympathy for Lucrece's own view of her plight as an irrevocable and intolerable state of shame is formed by the poem's skillful demonstration that her condition, post-rape, is one of simultaneous purity and filth – and, moreover, that the tension between the two cannot hold. Only in death can Lucrece remain both raped and chaste, both defiled and clean: were she to live, filth would obliterate purity.

Houen's paradigm of how a literary text "performs affects in an illocutionary fashion ... by structuring its emotional content in terms of what its formal devices are doing" is instructional here: the formal efforts that *The Rape of Lucrece* devotes to performing sympathy for Lucrece's shame make for a close parallel, in fact, with Houen's reading of shame and sympathy in a much later text concerned with the loss of chastity: Nathaniel Hawthorne's *The Scarlet Letter*. Hawthorne's narrator begins the novel by discovering the eponymous symbol of Hester's shame and "experienc[ing] a sensation not altogether physical, yet almost so... as if the letter were not of red cloth, but red-hot iron"; the narrator's affective experience is identified with Hester's experience of wearing the letter, which "brand[s] itself afresh into her soul" when others see it for the first time, and that "not altogether physical" sensation of "red-hot iron" is thus identified with the burning blush of shame. The narrator's sympathetic shame then structures a narrative that performs the same affect for the reader: "sympathy is what the narrator performs in reading Hester's character for the reader, and that performance is enhanced with the use of indirect discourse which acts to blend her voice with his. In other words, Hawthorne does everything to have the text reflexively structure for the reader an experience of sympathy so that the novel itself can exert the kind of quasi-physical feelings that its scarlet letter impresses upon the narrator and Hester."[53] But Hester, unlike Lucrece, experiences the straightforward and "justified" shame of a willing adulteress: regardless of the novel's critique of the inhumanity and hypocrisy of seventeenth-century American Puritanism, there is no dispute that

---

[52] Dubrow, *Captive Victors*, pp. 128, 80–82. [53] Houen, "Introduction," 225.

its protagonist has committed an act that she herself, the other characters in the
novel, Hawthorne, and his nineteenth-century audience all recognize as a sin,
however understandable and forgivable it might be. As stated earlier, however,
Shakespeare is writing within a Christian tradition that condemned suicide as
the mortal sin of despair, a tradition that could and did distance itself from
Lucrece as an example of misguided shame, based in the pagan overvaluing of
reputation. He thus needs to make his readers feel Lucrece's shame, and feel it to
be intolerable, in a way that to some extent overrides, at least on an affective
level, doctrinal scruples about taking one's own life. To perform sympathy for
the innocent, non-consenting Lucrece, structuring an experience of her shame
that transmits to the reader in a "quasi-physical" fashion, *The Rape of Lucrece*
relies on evoking the reader's disgust.

  Shakespeare's poem rejects Augustine's suggestion that Lucrece's suicide
may well have been a form of self-punishment for her sin of consent; it also,
however, rejects Augustine's arguably more progressive position (at least in
the abstract) that chastity is entirely a state of mind.[54] Lucrece herself declares
her mind to still be "Immaculate and spotless" (1654) after the rape, and the
narrator gives no reason for the reader to think otherwise.[55] However, the
moment where Lucrece gestures toward an anachronistically Christian view
on suicide – "'To kill myself,' quoth she, 'alack what were it, / But with my
body my poor soul's pollution?'" – is also the poem's clearest statement that
in the case of female sexual pollution, consent is irrelevant, because the mind
and soul, however spotless, are tainted *by the body*:

> "My body or my soul, which was the dearer.
> When the one pure, the other made divine?
> Whose love of either to myself was nearer,
> When both were kept for heaven and Collatine?
> Ay me, the bark pilled from the lofty pine,
> His leaves will wither and his sap decay;
> So must my soul, her bark being pilled away.

[54] Greenstadt, *Rise of the Author*, p.71.

[55] All references to *The Rape of Lucrece*, hereafter cited parenthetically by line
number, are to the New Cambridge Shakespeare, edited by John Roe.

"Her house is sacked, her quiet interrupted
Her mansion batt'red by the enemy;
Her sacred temple spotted, spoiled, corrupted,
Grossly engirt with daring infamy.
Then let it not be called impiety,
If in this blemished fort I make some hole,
Through which I may convey this troubled soul. (1163–1176)

Lucrece's argument here is that permitting her soul to live on within a polluted body would lead to the soul's contamination: her soul, still only "troubled" in the immediate aftermath of the rape, will "decay" and eventually come to resemble the body in which it resides – "spotted, spoiled, corrupted ... blemished" – just as the pine's leaves and sap gradually take on the same state as its ruined, barkless trunk. When she later faces her husband and father to ask how "this forcèd stain" might be "wiped" off of her, Lucrece already knows the answer: her "pure mind" cannot "with the foul act dispense," because the spoilage works in the other direction, from body to mind, making "foul" what is "pure" (1701, 1704). The lines that raise the possibility of such purification are structured to imply that nobody, neither Lucrece nor the men, truly believes in it:

"May my pure mind with the foul act dispense,
My low-declinèd honour to advance?
May any terms acquit me from this chance?
The poisoned fountain clears itself again;
And why not I from this compellèd stain?"

With this they all at once began to say
Her body's stain her mind untainted clears;
While with a joyless smile she turns away
That face, that map which deep impression bears
Of hard misfortune, carved in it with tears. (1704–1713)

By having the men fall over each other "all at once" to agree with the implied logic of Lucrece's devil's-advocate rhetorical question only *after* such logic has been supplied for them, the poem undermines any sense that they genuinely subscribe to it; Lucrece's response to their effusions, as she looks away with "a joyless smile" (1711), shows that she doesn't either.[56] Shakespeare's *Lucrece* brings its readers to feel for and with a woman whose mind and soul are yet pure, but whose bodily pollution is so real, and so overwhelming, that it is slowly seeping into every part of her being, a psycho-physiological condition that produces unbearable shame.

My argument for how the language of Shakespeare's poem performs sympathy for Lucrece through performing disgust will work backward from the poem's hints at Lucrece's involuntary pleasure during the rape. Given early modern beliefs about female pleasure and conception, this possibility would have been coded for early modern readers in her fear that Tarquin's "bastard graff" may be growing inside her, "pollut[ing]" Collatine's "stock" in that word's double sense of "tree trunk" (Lucrece herself, into whom the bastard has been grafted) and "descendants."[57] The pollution of pleasure is twofold, both the literal, continued presence of Tarquin's seed in her womb – seed that would have been transient had her own seed-producing sexual response not created the fertile conditions for it to remain and grow – and the prurient assumption that the excitements of illicit intercourse leave a woman helplessly wanting more of the same. In John Fletcher's *The Tragedy of Valentinian*, Maximus worries that if his wife Lucina were to outlive her rape by the emperor Valentinian, their descendants would inevitably conclude as much: "when they read she lived, / Must they not ask how often she was ravished / And make a doubt she

---

[56] Both Belsey, "Tarquin Dispossessed," 331–332, and Maus, "Tropes," 69–71, see the men as sincere in this passage, and Lucrece's refusal to accept their reasoning as female self-determination; both offer illuminating readings of Lucrece's sense that her tainted body will damage her soul, but see this dilemma largely in psychological, not physical, terms.

[57] Baines, "Effacing Rape," 88. On Lucrece's pleasure as a "common speculation" in retellings of the tale, see also Donaldson, *Rapes of Lucretia*, pp. 36–37, and Sanchez, *Erotic Subjects*, pp. 93–94.

loved that more than wedlock?" (3.1.242–245). In Coluccio Salutati's early fifteenth-century *Declamatio Lucretiae*, Lucretia herself, tormented by the memory of her "unpleasing pleasure," spells out the logic of this process as she explains why she must die:

> Allow me not to harbor so much grief in my soul and not to recall so much the feeling of that embrace without the enticements of my disobedient members assailing me, without remembering the traces of the marriage flame . . . . [T]oo great are the powers of Venus for anyone who has had some experience of pleasure. . . . Nothing softens grief and emotions in a woman more quickly than time which extinguishes them; if I delay, perhaps shameful acts will begin to please me. Let me pierce with a sword this breast which that violent one loved, feeling first my nipples with his fingers impressed for the purpose of inciting lust. Don't even wish me to feel compassion for myself. If I spare adultery, soon adultery will be pleasing, and then an adulterer will be welcome. A disgraceful thing has begun in me.[58]

In Shakespeare's poem, this kind of thinking is arguably the most likely subtext behind Lucrece's assertion that her polluted body cannot help but destroy the chastity of her soul, that the "pill[ing] away" of her body's purity will lead inexorably to her soul's "decay" (1168–1169). The poem, after all, has already informed its readers about "weak-made" women's "waxen minds," which are susceptible to taking – indeed, unable *not* to take – "th'impression of strange kinds / . . . formed in them by force, by fraud, or skill" (1260, 1240–1243). Read in the light of these admissions, the narrator's statement directly after the rape – "She bears the load of lust he left behind / And he the burden of a guilty mind" (734–735) – is an explicit demonstration of Lucrece's pollution through unchaste, involuntary pleasure. With "the load of lust," the poem compresses four interrelated

---

[58] The full text of Salutati's *Declamatio Lucretiae* is translated in Jed, *Chaste Thinking*, pp. 149–152; see p. 151.

meanings into one alliterative phrase: in its most metaphorical, least material meaning, Tarquin's lust has left Lucrece with the load of grief, guilt, shame, dishonor, and everything else she suffers before she takes her own life. In its most material sense, though, the line presents the reader with the disgust-substance of nonmarital, unwanted semen: lust has made him ejaculate his seminal "load" into her body. Between the two lie the insidious implications of the effect Tarquin's fluids have on their unwilling recipient: a woman "bear[ing]" a "load" evokes the bearing of children, which takes the trope back to pregnancy and the female pleasure required for conception, a pleasure commonly believed to be enhanced, or even produced, by precisely that literal "load," the woman's reception of the man's seed.[59] The fourth and final meaning is hiding in plain sight: if Tarquin leaves Lucrece bearing a load of lust, then Lucrece *now has lust*. Against her will, through the involuntary excitement pruriently assumed to occur during a rape, the chaste wife has been made *lustful*.

Beneath the shame of Lucrece's unwanted pleasure and its effects, then, lies a subtle invitation to regard the newly polluted Lucrece with disgust. Returning to the material meaning of this "load of lust" – namely, the seminal fluid evoked most literally a few stanzas earlier to mark the actual moment of intercourse – "O that prone lust should stain so pure a bed! / The spots whereof could weeping purify / Her tears should drop on them perpetually" (684–686) – Lucrece's contamination by Tarquin goes beyond the revulsion, familiar enough to the modern reader, at the "stain[s]" and "spots" of semen here presented as if soiling the bedsheets, to include a distressingly thoroughgoing state of internal filth. Catherine Belling's work on blood and bloodletting in *The Rape of Lucrece* offers a fascinating reading of how Tarquin's corrupted, plethoric blood enters Lucrece's body through his semen to infect her own blood with a condition known as *cacochymia*. This term, as defined by Nicholas Gyer in *The English Phlebotomy* (1592), refers to "all corruption of humors in quality: whereby the powers of the bodie are hindered from their proper functions, whereby

---

[59] On the belief that male ejaculation was pleasurable for women, see Panek, "Base Stallion Trade," 366–367.

also the whole bodie waxeth filthie and daily decayeth."[60] As Belling
explains:

> Female chastity contaminated by dishonorable sex was
> a condition both literally and figuratively similar to the
> corruption of the blood by cacochymia. It was literal to
> the extent that (hetero) sexual intercourse more or less
> always involved the introduction of the man's blood into
> the female body, for sperm is made of blood. Virtuous sex,
> within marriage, meant the sharing of well-governed blood;
> blood conveyed during illegitimate sex was of necessity
> corrupted by the act (and usually, as in Tarquin's case,
> distilled from already imperfect blood, part of the condition
> causing that act), and this corrupt blood was left in the body
> of the woman, to breed disease and bastards – infection and
> infestation.[61]

There is thus a literal element to the poem's images of phlebotomy, from
Lucrece's assertion that "The remedy indeed to do [her] good / Is to let
forth [her] foul defilèd blood" (1028–1029), to the elaborate, quasi-medical
description of the blood that issues from her stab wound "In two slow
rivers": one "pure and red," the other "black" and described over the course
of eight lines as "stained," "tainted," "corrupted," and "putrified" (1743–
1750).[62] Belling's focus is on disease, but the language of filth and rot
surrounding "corrupted" blood in contemporary medical texts like Gyer's
strikingly evokes how this substance is not just diseased but disgusting: with
corrupted blood, "the whole body waxeth filthie and daily decayeth" (8);
corruption may be accompanied by "rottennes and putrifaction" (9); elsewhere in the text, "corruption," "rottenness," and "putrefaction" are used
as virtual synonyms, as when Gyer recommends bloodletting for "corruption and putrefaction of bloud and humors in the veynes without plenitude,
called *Cacochymia*" (112) or, in the case of certain fevers, recommends it to

---

[60] Quoted in Belling, "Infectious Rape," 117–118.
[61] Belling, "Infectious Rape," 119. [62] Ibid., 119, 121–123.

relieve "abundance," when "the rottenness or putrefaction of the humor [is] without the veynes" (117). Corrupted blood can even, in rare cases, "stinke," and "if it doo, the same sheweth corrupt and stinking humours, and is a token of incurable putrefaction and corruption."[63] Quoting the final description of Lucrece's bleeding, in which her "blood untainted still doth red abide / Blushing at that which is so putrified" (1749–1750), Belling notes how it recalls Lucrece's own earlier blushes, which signified "both innocence and shame": "the very purity of her 'untainted' blood is evinced by the red blush with which it responds to the disgrace from which it can now at last flow apart. The separation of self from sin that finally becomes possible for her blood is achieved at the cost of Lucrece's own bodily integrity."[64] The blush of innocence separating itself from disgrace and sin, however, surely goes hand in hand with the blush of shame at having just recently mingled with something so revoltingly "putrified."

If Lucrece's pollution ends with a clotting pool of rotten blood, it begins with a passage that even more graphically engages the reader's disgust. Coloring the reader's view of Lucrece directly after the rape, the first affective response to the attack is not Lucrece's distress or even her shame, but Tarquin's nauseated satiation:

> Look as the full-fed hound or gorged hawk,
> Unapt for tender smell or speedy flight,
> Make slow pursuit, or altogether balk
> The prey wherein by nature they delight,
> So surfeit-taking Tarquin fares this night.
> His taste delicious, in digestion souring,
> Devours his will that lived by foul devouring.

---

[63] Gyer, *English Phlebotomy*, p. 257. Gyer's text in fact says "It is sildome, that the bloud comming from the veines, doth sinke" but "sinke" appears to be a misprint for "stinke": see Harward, *Phlebotomy*, p. 125, who borrows from Gyer, but revises this line to "If the bloud doe smell ill (as it falleth out but seldome) it is a signe of a very great putrefaction."

[64] Belling, "Infectious Rape," 122–123.

O deeper sin than bottomless conceit
Can comprehend in still imagination!
Drunken Desire must vomit his receipt
Ere he can see his own abomination. (694–704)

The disgust of surfeit is different from the disgust related to contamination in that the contaminated substance is disgusting to anyone aware of the contamination, while the substance that provokes surfeit is disgusting only to the surfeiter; however, the turn to Tarquin's viewpoint, the viscerally familiar sensation of "balking" at that which seemed "delicious" before we "gorged" on it, and the fact that disgust requires an object, combine to present Lucrece herself – the food on which Tarquin has gorged himself – as having been rendered disgusting.[65] And since Lucrece is also "Drunken Desire['s] . . . receipt," or the drink with which Tarquin has inebriated himself to the point of surfeit, then she is also what he – and the reader – "sees," in a vilely transformed state, when the drunkard faces his own vomit in the last two lines of the passage quoted above. Her feeling of her own filthiness is then picked up as soon as the poem turns to her viewpoint. After a moment in which she "lies panting" like a lamb attacked by a "thievish dog," her next action seems to be a frantic attempt to cleanse herself: "She, desperate, with her nails her flesh doth tear" (739). But no amount of cleansing can make appetizing the now-loathed food or drink on which one has surfeited to the point of vomiting, let alone purify the pool of vomit itself. Nor can the intellectual acknowledgment of Lucrece's guiltless non-consent and her heroic self-sacrifice, both before and after the rape, for her family's honor, fully override the reader's visceral sense that in Lucrece's defiled condition, the "helpless shame" (756) she experiences is no more than the natural and justified response.

---

[65] On the "intentionality" of disgust – i.e., its direction toward an object – see Korsmeyer, *Savoring Disgust*, pp.16–17, 36–37; Ahmed, *Cultural Politics*, p. 85; Miller *Anatomy*, p. 8. On the specific disgust provoked by surfeit, both sexual and gustatory, see Miller, *Anatomy*, pp. 120–127; McGinn, *Meaning of Disgust*, pp. 120–127.

   Christopher Tilmouth's account of the relation between pollution and shame in *The Rape of Lucrece* posits Lucrece's shame itself as the polluting substance:

> Lucrece's anxiety is that her soul, set with in a now 'poison'd closet" (1658), "Grossly engirt with . . . infamy' (1173), and perhaps even scarred on its outside, like a 'sacred temple . . . spoil'd' (1172), will itself become subject to that seeping bodily pollution currently staining its extremities. Physically and psychologically, shame threatens to inundate Lucrece's consciousness, overwhelming whatever contrary, more positive self-image she yet retains. This threat arises because Lucrece senses a degree of complicity in her own rape without being able to determine that complicity's limits.

While I agree with Tilmouth's assessment of the factors contributing to Lucrece's "unquantifiable guilt," which range from her irrational self-blame at not having resisted sufficiently to her loss of innocence and forced awakening to "the primal sin of carnality," his claim that Lucrece's self-imposed task is "to halt and reverse shame's polluting ingress into her soul" would seem to conflate cause with effect.[66] As I have been arguing, her shame is not itself the pollutant, but instead an affective response to being forcibly, physically polluted, a response that does not depend on a guilty sense of complicity, although such feelings may well be an exacerbating factor. Some rather unlikely illumination on this particular relation between disgust and shame can be gleaned from Miller's discussion of medieval Icelandic sagas and a practice in which one feuding group would hold a three-day siege of the other's dwellings for the sole purpose of preventing their enemies from accessing their outhouses, thus forcing them to defecate indoors and live amid their own dirt: "Clearly defecation is degrading and contaminating. It is hedged in with rules about appropriateness as to place. . . . Disgust and shame work in tandem here. To defecate inside is shameful because it forces people to violate disgust norms in a setting where

---

[66] Tilmouth, "Open Consciences," 508–509.

such violation shames them. The shame is twofold: it is the shame of being coerced and beaten in the give-and-take of feud, and it is the shame of being forced to do something disgusting."[67] The setting in which the violation of disgust norms produces shame clearly has to do with both the forcing, inflicted by another, and the knowledge held by that other (or by multiple others), inseparable from the forcing, of one's coerced disgustingness. Presumably, if a medieval Icelander were to lock himself in his own house by accident and need to defecate indoors, unbeknownst to anyone else, he would feel plenty of disgust but little to no shame. Lucrece, however, not only knows that Tarquin knows, but is convinced that anyone who looks at her will instantly know as well:

"Make me not object to the tell-tale Day:
The light will show, charactered in my brow,
The story of sweet chastity's decay,
The impious breach of holy wedlock vow.
Yea, the illiterate, that know not how
To cipher what is writ in learnèd books,
Will quote my loathsome trespass in my looks. (806–812)

While the central metaphor here is Lucrece as a written "story," legible to all, the opposition in "*sweet* chastity's *decay*" brings out the phrase's material implications of fragrance and wholesomeness turned to malodorous rot, coloring – or, more accurately, scenting – the *loathsome* of the final line.

The specifically sexual nature, however, of Lucrece's pollution brings it into relation with shame in an insidious way that has no parallel in Icelandic forced-defecation sieges. A significant part of Lucrece's shame in having her pollution known is that it sexualizes her in the eyes of others: that men, in particular, will see her and imagine her being raped. The poem evokes this facet of Lucrece's excruciating shame through two contrasting encounters with the first people to see her in her tainted condition: a female servant, and then a male one. Facing the first woman she meets after the rape, Lucrece is

[67] Miller, *Anatomy*, pp. 147–148.

pale and weeping – her "cheeks unto her maid seem so / As winter meads when sun doth melt their snow" (1217–1218) – and her sorrow is met with the maid's own empathetic tears. Facing the first man, however, the awkward groom who will deliver her letter to Collatine, pale, cold sorrow is replaced with an ever-intensifying series of mutual hot blushes when Lucrece misreads the groom's reddened face of "bashful innocence" (1341) as revealing his awareness of what Tarquin has done to her: "But they whose guilt within their bosoms lie / Imagine every eye beholds their blame; / For Lucrece thought he blushed to see her shame" (1342–1344). Her response to his blush is her own deepening sense of shame at being seen in her new, "blemished" state:

> His kindled duty kindled her mistrust,
> That two red fires in both their faces blazèd;
> She thought he blushed, as knowing Tarquin's lust,
> And blushing with him, wistly on him gazèd;
> Her earnest eye did make him more amazèd;
> The more she saw the blood his cheeks replenish,
> The more she thought he spied in her some blemish. (1352–1358)

When Lucrece thinks the groom blushes "*as knowing* Tarquin's lust," the ambiguity of the phrasing brings two shameful possibilities – one perhaps inseparable from the other – into play: when a man looks at the raped Lucrece, *knowing* that she has experienced "Tarquin's lust," he may also respond by *knowing* "Tarquin's lust," in the sense that thinking about Lucrece being sexually used by Tarquin causes him to experience similar lust himself. The heat and engorgement of the "red fire" that blazes in the man's face and the pumping blood that visibly "replenishes" his cheeks are thus as likely to be the flush of sexual arousal as the "modest Compassion" that brings on a blush in an empathetic person who "observes ought in another, deserving blame."[68] In Lucrece's imagining of what the groom is

---

[68] Brathwaite, *English Gentlewoman*, p. 168. Brathwaite is talking about women in this passage, and given that Shakespeare's narrator has just associated emotional empathy with the "gentle sex" who "Griev[e] . . . . themselves to guess at others'

imagining, the statement that she "thought he blushed to see her shame" (1344) may even take on an additional, unbearable implication: as he blushes (or so she thinks) at her shameful condition, he is also "seeing," in his mind's eye, her "shame," or genitalia, exposed in the act of rape (*OED*, "shame" n. 7) – a sight that, once again, calls the nature of his blush / flush into question.[69] It takes a bad man like Tarquin to think of Collatine's chaste wife as a sexual object and be aroused at the thought of sullying her purity; *Measure for Measure's* Angelo is cut from similar cloth. But what man, the poem implies, can refrain from thinking about Lucrece as a sexual object – *someone's* sexual object, even if not his – once sullied purity has become her defining feature? When Lucrece, a moment before she stabs herself, seems to explain her suicide as a posthumous policing of other women's chastity – "no dame hereafter living / By my excuse shall claim excuse's giving" (1714–1715) – her concerns may also be more immediate and personal: if Lucrece lives, she lives knowing that her rape is being repeatedly reimagined, brought before men's eyes every time a woman excuses her own illicit sexual encounter – nonconsensual or otherwise – by invoking Lucrece's defilement in order to claim for herself that "her body's stain her mind untainted clears" (1710).[70]

smarts" (1237–1238), one wonders whether empathetic shame *would* be an expected male response in a man who *did* know Lucrece had submitted to "Tarquin's lust."

[69] After all, the poem has already shown its reader this sight in lines 679–681: see Fineman, "Shakespeare's Will," 43, who points out the "smirky collation of Lucrece's mouth with her vagina" when Tarquin "entombs her outcry in her lips' sweet fold."

[70] Daileader, "Writing Rape," 75, calls this statement about other women the "aspect of Lucrece's characterization by Shakespeare that I find hardest, as a feminist, to stomach. . . . Lucrece kills herself, in effect, so that other raped women will also kill themselves." While I don't disagree, it's worth considering Lucrece's horror of being "made a theme for disputation" and having her name linked with Tarquin's even in tales that focus on *his* shame (822, 813–819). To live at all is to live with the knowledge of other people's knowledge.

By suggesting that the thought of Lucrece's "stained" body is titillating to men – titillating precisely *because* it has been dirtied – *The Rape of Lucrece* enters the territory of what Kolnai terms "the eroticism of disgust." As Korsmeyer elaborates,

> The intentional structure of this emotion is directed so strongly toward the properties of the disgusting object that it rivets our attention, even at the same time that it repels. This aversion actually searches out its object. In Kolnai's vivid metaphor, the tip of the arrow of intentionality "penetrates the object," thus making this aversion paradoxically caressing and probing. This may be the root of the attraction of disgust, for "there is already in its inner logic a possibility of a positive laying hold of the object, whether by touching, consuming, or embracing it." . . . [Kolnai] recognizes a perverse magnetism, what he calls "the eroticism of disgust," in which aversion is superimposed "upon the shadow of a desire for union with the object."[71]

Kolnai's example of this "eroticism," interestingly, is not sexual but culinary: the "delicately equivocal evaluation" involved in enjoying "penetratingly smelly cheeses" that are all the more enticing for their tinge of putrefaction.[72] For a culture where nonmarital sex of any kind transforms the woman's body into an object of disgust – a privy, a rotten orange, tainted meat, a spider-contaminated glass of wine, a cistern full of slippery toads – the newly, unwillingly polluted Lucrece has just enough of a tinge of that disgust-quality to be fascinating, even delectable. "Although there is a change of affect from recoil to savor, the shadow of the former lingers: indeed, it is in that shadow that the sophisticated depth of flavor resides. On the other hand, though the sensation has shifted only a little, the affective response has radically altered, having switched from recoil to appetite. Disgust has been replaced by savoring."[73] This is Korsmeyer on "the sensory family resemblance" between the vileness of milk gone bad and

---

[71] Korsmeyer, *Savoring Disgust*, p. 37. [72] Kolnai, *Disgust*, p. 60.
[73] Korsmeyer, *Savoring Disgust*, p. 65.

the deliciousness of cheese; is it too much of a stretch to see, as well, a provocative description of the resemblance between a willing adulteress or prostitute and the newly raped Lucrece? To the extent that readers have found Shakespeare's *Lucrece* to be an erotic, even pornographic text, its lengthy "caressing and probing" of the physical and emotional state of a woman whose sexual purity is just a little tainted, and still in the earliest stages of decay, may well contribute to its eroticism.[74]

Women Beware Women

What, though, if the raped wife insists on living? What if instead of killing herself she makes the pragmatic and unspectacular choice of accepting the consolation prize of wealth, power, and protection that her powerful rapist offers as compensation for her lost chastity? This is the experiment on the classic rape scenario that Middleton performs in the main plot of *Women Beware Women*; it may also be the reason why numerous readers – both literary critics and theater directors – have assumed that Bianca is not raped but seduced. With Lucrece furnishing the dominant paradigm for rape in early modern tragedy, the sacrificial suicide of the chaste rape victim is so axiomatic that "without the woman's self-slaughter there is no rape."[75] In an early feminist article situating *Women Beware Women* within a series of other contemporary plays involving rape, Suzanne Gossett separates these plays into two clusters: an earlier group that features the traditional pattern of the rape of a married woman, her suicide, and her male relatives' revenge; and a later one that rings changes on this pattern, including the victim's marriage to her assailant. In *Women Beware Women*,

> As in the earlier plays, a married woman is raped by the state's most powerful man, in this case the Duke of Florence. . . . Confronted in a private gallery by the Duke,

---

[74] For readings that criticize *Lucrece* for eroticizing the rape and mitigating Tarquin's crime, see Smith, "Exonerating Rape," and Hall, "Lewd but Familiar Eyes."

[75] Little, *Shakespeare Jungle Fever*, p. 28.

> Bianca is in precisely the same situation as Lucina in
> [Beaumont and Fletcher's *The Tragedy of*] *Valentinian*,
> also tricked to the palace and suddenly confronted by the
> Emperor. . . . The innovations begin not in the rape scene
> but thereafter, when none of the principals behaves accord-
> ing to the pattern.[76]

My focus in this section will be on one of the first and most often overlooked of these innovations – namely, Bianca's immediate reaction upon returning to the stage after the rape – where the scene directs the audience's disgust not toward the defiled victim, as in Shakespeare's *Rape of Lucrece*, but toward the man who has forced himself upon her. As with *Lucrece*, the feeling in question is physical, visceral disgust, not merely moral disapproval. Bianca's disgust reaction to the Duke, I will argue, lends affective justification to her failure to react to rape with the conventionally virtuous response of blushing shame, and to her defiant, even "shameless" performance of the role she has been forced to assume. Making the audience feel the Duke's rape of Bianca as not only reprehensible but repulsive – making them feel *her* repulsion – is one powerful way in which modern productions can represent Bianca's notoriously problematic transformation into her rapist's venal mistress without reproducing what Kim Solga terms the "spectacular . . . disappearance of violence against women in early modern performance." In *Women Beware Women*, the Duke's violent sexual assault on Bianca is erased *as* a violent assault when it is represented as resulting in her desire for him, and in the conventional pairing of female beauty and male power: the powerful man who has won a desirable young woman away from his undeserving inferior.[77] As Gossett observes, "One popular theory has always held that women enjoy fantasies of being sexually overpowered, and Bianca is drawn by the very power that the Duke has expressed through rape."[78] When *Women Beware Women* is staged in ways that foreground the play's cues for disgust, such "theories" about female desire are exposed for the dangerous fictions they are.

[76] Gossett, "Marrying the Rapist," 319. [77] Solga, *Violence Against Women*, p. 1.
[78] Gossett, "Marrying the Rapist," 320.

That Middleton writes the encounter between Bianca and the Duke to be staged as a rape, not a seduction, seems to me incontrovertible.[79] Arguments that the scene depicts a seduction tend to be based in inferences about Bianca's psychology: her supposed desire for the wealth and luxuries she has renounced to marry Leantio, which is then back-read onto her sudden demands, following her encounter with the Duke, for goods the Mother cannot afford; her lack of sexual fulfillment during her husband's absence; her willfulness and/or lustfulness, as evinced by her decision to elope in the first place. Such arguments, as I will discuss, also tend to read an undertone of sexual interest into her first sighting of the Duke during the annual progress she watches from her window. Joost Daalder's recent defense of the "seduction" reading insists that "much of our understanding, particularly of Bianca's state of mind before and after this episode, can only be derived from equally thorough analysis of earlier and later parts of the play."[80] Playgoers at a performance, however, are unlikely to be analyzing Bianca's earlier state of mind as they watch what happens to her in Livia's picture gallery, and they have no access to her later one. As I will demonstrate, the evidence that what they are watching is a rape – and, as Gossett has argued, a fairly traditional one at that – is not psychological but situational, not to be found in holistically derived deductions about

[79] Critics writing before the mid-1980s routinely assume the encounter to be a seduction; the most thorough analysis of the scene as seduction (and the most sympathetic to Bianca) is Foster, "The Deed's Creature," 511–513. Arguments for rape seem to have begun with Gossett, "Marrying the Rapist," followed by Dawson, "Economy of Rape," Hotz-Davies, "Feminism," 35–37, and Daileader, *Eroticism*, pp. 25–28; that Bianca is raped is taken as a given by Williams, "Silence," 106. By the mid 1990s, critics who wanted to treat the scene as a seduction had to counter the rape arguments: see Biggs, "Does the Duke Rape Bianca?" 97–100; Biggs' claims for seduction are rebutted by Hutchings, "Rape, Seduction, or Power?" 366–367. The seduction argument was revived at length in 2011 by Daalder, "State of the Art," 84–88. For arguments that the nature of the encounter is left uncertain, see Heller, "Space, Violence and Bodies," 428–432, and Detmer-Goebel, "Dramatizing Consent," 153–156.

[80] Daalder, "State of the Art," 88.

Bianca's state of mind, but clearly indicated by the action and dialogue immediately before and after the offstage sexual act takes place.

The scene's parallels to undisputed rape scenarios familiar to early modern audiences go beyond the echo of *Valentinian*, noted by Gossett, in Bianca being tricked into the Duke's grasp. The Duke, like Tarquin in Shakespeare's *The Rape of Lucrece* (645–648), declares himself sexually excited by his victim's verbal resistance, a point he makes not once but twice: "The lifting of thy voice is but like one / That does exalt his enemy, who, proving high / Lays all the plots to confound him that raised him"; "Thou know'st the way to please me. I affect / A passionate pleading 'bove an easy yielding, / But never pitied any" (2.2.336–338, 359–361).[81] The Duke, like the emperor Valentinian, and like the Duchess's son in *The Revenger's Tragedy* (1.4.42), employs panders to procure his victim and facilitate the rape: Bianca denounces Livia as a "pandress" (4.1.73) and a "bawd" (2.2.464; 4.1.74), and curses Guardiano for having "abased" her and made her fit "for use" (2.2.436). The Duke, like the Tyrant in Middleton's *The Lady's Tragedy*, and again, like Valentinian, tries to buy his victim's consent with promises of wealth and favor. Valentinian offers Lucina "jewels," "honours" (1.1.33–35), and much more in exchange for her chastity, rapes her when these offers prove futile, and then renews the offers after the rape, promising to "ever love and honour [her]" (3.1.19) and to make her "the mightiest / More than myself" (3.1.114–115) if she becomes his mistress. The Tyrant in Middleton's *The Lady's Tragedy* offers the betrothed Lady the chance to become one of the "feathered mistresses / That glister in the sun of prince's favours" (2.1.71–72), and sends a jewel, a pander, and a gang of soldiers as his final effort: the jewel and the pander to win the Lady over, and the soldiers to seize her for him to rape should the jewel fail. The Duke, if anything, is a *more* determined rapist than either Valentinian or the Tyrant, making his offer of "wealth, honour ... [and] a duke's favour" (2.2.369–370) as an afterthought rather than an opening gambit. Within three lines of his entrance, he physically seizes Bianca and gropes her breasts – "Prithee, tremble not; / I feel thy breast shake like

[81] Hotz-Davies, "Feminism," 36, lists these passages to show that the Duke "seems to get a special satisfaction" out of Bianca's resistance.

a turtle panting / Under a loving hand that makes much on't" (2.2.320–322) –
and his next speech indicates that his bodily restraint of her will last for the
duration of their time on stage together:

> Pish, strive not, sweet!
> This strength were excellent employed in love, now,
> But here 'tis spent amiss. Strive not to seek
> Thy liberty and keep me still in prison.
> I'faith, you shall not out till I'm released now;
> We'll be both freed together, or stay still by't;
> So is captivity pleasant. (2.2.333)[82]

Construing his grasp on Bianca as a "prison" and "captivity," he states that
he will not release her until she provides his sexual release. There is nothing
in the rest of the scene to indicate that he goes back on this assertion and
releases his grasp before he exits the stage with her. His threat, some ten
lines later, of "I should be sorry the least force should lay / An unkind
touch upon thee" (2.2.344–345) is not evidence that he has let go of her in
the meantime, as it is perfectly clear that the Duke does not consider his
restraint and groping of the struggling Bianca "an unkind touch": to his
mind, it is "pleasant" captivity and "a loving hand that makes much"
(2.2.322) of her body.[83] This is a man who is there to take what he wants,
on the spot, whether or not Bianca wishes to profit from it later: "I am not
here in vain," he states bluntly; "have but the leisure / to think on that, and
thou't soon be resolved" (2.2.334–335).

---

[82] Daileader, *Eroticism*, p. 27, pays close attention to the Duke's physical restraint of
Bianca.

[83] Biggs, "Does the Duke Rape Bianca?" 98, claims that "there is no evidence that
the Duke is still restraining her physically" after line 344; he quotes the Duke's
"you shall not out till I'm released," but does not consider its implications for
staging. Heller, "Space, Violence and Bodies," 431, reiterates Biggs' claim,
reading the Duke's line about the "unkind touch" as evidence that "the text does
not indicate any more physical contact."

At this point we might consider Emily Detmer-Goebel's intriguing argument that rape, in early modern England, would have been legally defined by the victim's actions *after* the act rather than by anything she or the perpetrator may have said or done before and during: "Bianca's actions after the Duke's entrapment now imply 'consent after,' transforming rape into an adulterous relationship. Although it was against her will, Bianca apparently accepts the Duke's offer."[84] Legal definitions, however, are not always consonant with literary or theatrical representations, and *Valentinian*, once again, provides an illuminating comparison. Informed of Lucina's death, Valentinian rages against his panders for having misled him: "You would work wonders; / There was no chastity above your practice; / You would undertake to make her love her wrongs / And dote upon her rape" (4.1.7–8). In Valentinian's fantasy, the raped Lucina agrees to become his wealthy, powerful mistress – that is, she does what Bianca does – and she comes to love the rape that brought about her fate. Even in this scenario, though, the rapist recognizes that subsequent actions do not transform the original events: the wrongs remain wrongs, and the rape remains rape.

The argument for "consent after" also overlooks the extraordinary constraints, both real and perceived, on Bianca's actions immediately following the assault. Detmer-Goebel states that "Although [Bianca] speaks bitterly, significantly, she does not raise hue and cry, nor claim rape. Rather than re-presenting what has happened to her as rape, she hides her shame and appears 'lively' and 'cheerful' in front of her mother-in-law."[85] To whom, though, is Bianca to raise the hue and cry? Raped by the ruler, she has no higher authority to whom she can appeal. Moreover, the play

---

[84] Detmer-Goebel, "Dramatizing Consent," 155. A thorough analysis of the early modern shift from rape as a property crime to rape as a crime against a person – and how the concomitant emphasis on consent did not necessarily benefit women – is provided by Dolan, "Re-reading Rape," 8–10.

[85] Detmer-Goebel, "Dramatizing Consent," 155. Solga, *Violence against Women*, pp. 36–40, illuminates how the hue and cry required of rape victims was a carefully scripted performance to be enacted before a specific audience of witnesses: Bianca (who is not discussed by Solga) has no audience before whom to perform.

strongly implies that Bianca believes her mother-in-law to be complicit with the panders.[86] In the Duke's final speech before he takes Bianca offstage, his promises of wealth and honor – the promises that the "seduction" critics see as motivating her capitulation – are accompanied by the assurance that Bianca's "own mother" would approve of their liaison; he also reveals knowledge of her marital and economic circumstances that only Leantio's mother could have divulged.[87] If, at this point, Bianca stops struggling and resigns herself to the assault, her sudden realization that even the Mother will not protect her is a more likely reason than any attraction to what the Duke has to offer. Bianca has been aware from the start of the play that the Mother fears she will not be satisfied with their relative poverty (1.1.119–121); the Mother is the one who has brought her to Livia's house, despite Leantio's prohibition, and agreed that Guardiano should take her upstairs to show her "the monument" (2.2.279). Bianca thus has good reason to suspect that the Mother is involved in the scheme to hand her over to the Duke, whether for some immediate personal gain, or to procure a wealthy lover who will provide ongoing maintenance for a young woman she fears will be demanding. The Duke, after all, initially suggests that Bianca take him as a "friend" *in addition* to her husband (2.2.347–348); she would not have to leave her marriage to become his secret mistress. Even if Bianca were to escape the Duke's grasp and flee downstairs, what protection could she expect from the woman who has brought her there to be prostituted? Even if she were to escape Livia's house and return to her new home, what safety could she find there with Leantio away and the Mother holding the keys (1.1.176)? Understanding that Bianca believes her mother-in-law to have prostituted her to the Duke also makes a good deal of sense of her behavior

---

[86] This point is made by Levin, "Bianca Should Beware Mother," 371–389. Levin, however, also makes the untenable argument that the Mother *does* scheme with Guardiano and Livia to hand Bianca over to the Duke, ignoring the Mother's soliloquies in act three, scene one: both make it clear she knows nothing of what has transpired. The evidence that Bianca *thinks* she does is nonetheless compelling.

[87] "Mother" was commonly used for "mother-in-law," and is Bianca's normal term of address for Leantio's mother.

in the next scene, where her whole demeanor toward the Mother has changed – "She's grown so cutted, there's no speaking to her" (3.1.4) – and she demands silver-and-gilt casting bottles, green silk quilts, and other furnishings she knows the family cannot possibly afford. Proponents of the seduction argument tend to see this scene as revealing Bianca's true nature, and to take her apparent dissatisfaction with the Mother's house as evidence of her inherent susceptibility to the Duke's temptations.[88] Given that Bianca's transformation, however, involves both material demands *and* unconcealed animosity toward the woman she had earlier treated with loving respect, it is fair to see it as solidly and explicitly motivated by what she "learns" in the previous scene: if the Mother has turned her into a high-class courtesan, then the Mother, she insinuates, at least owes her the trappings that go with the position. Middleton's original audiences may well have been aware of his penchant for plots in which parents prostitute, or attempt to prostitute, their daughters, including *The Lady's Tragedy*, *The Revenger's Tragedy*, and *A Mad World, My Masters*; they thus would have noticed the pattern being evoked in *Women Beware Women*, this time with the tragic irony that Bianca is *not* caught up in the kind of Middletonian plot she thinks she is.

To take the scene in which the Duke begins his assault of Bianca – replete with echoes of known rape plots, not-so-veiled threats, forcible restraint, and assurances that resistance is not only futile for the victim but arousing for the assailant – and to stage it as a seduction, leading to Bianca's consent and/or exciting her sexual desire, is to perpetuate some very old stereotypes. As Solga observes, performance is "a means of cultural and historical intervention"; possibilities for intervention into the erasure of violence against women lie latent within certain early modern dramas, and are "manifested in contemporary performances of those dramas with greater or lesser degrees of success."[89] A 1994 production by the Buttonhole Theatre Company (dir. Christopher Geelan) in which Bianca was clearly seduced, not raped, emphasized the class difference between

---

[88] Biggs, "Does the Duke Rape Bianca?" 99; see also Daalder, "State of the Art," 87.

[89] Solga, *Violence against Women*, p. 3.

Leantio and his bride: played by Noma Dumezweni, this Bianca was an African princess who was markedly out of place in her new husband's social milieu; her seduction by the Duke, whose attentions she welcomed from the start, included "a strong sense of Bianca's return home in terms of class." While this characterization of Bianca certainly clarified her motivation, "[t]he suggestion that Bianca willingly consents to the Duke's demands in order to rehabilitate her social standing tend[ed] to flatten out both her character and the gender politics of the play."[90] Assuming no cuts were made to the Duke's lines, staging the scene as an unambiguous seduction would also present the language – and likely the physical behavior, too – of force and coercion as part of the excitement of adulterous courtship, naturalizing them as tools of a powerful man's sexual success. Such seems to have been the case in Jesse Berger's 2009 Red Bull production, which emphasized the darkly comic aspects of the play. A still of Bianca's encounter with the Duke shows Geraint Wyn Davies' left hand gripping Jennifer Ikeda's arm so hard that his fingers sink into her flesh, while she looks down in apparent perplexity at his right hand splayed over her breast; yet this Duke's aggressive advances were received by Bianca as a "welcome opportunity for swift social advancement," and "her protests quickly turn-[ed] to happy surrender."[91] On the other hand, playing up the scene's perceived complexities risks producing the same effect as flattening them into a simple seduction. Peter Smith's review of the Birmingham Repertory Theatre's 1989 *Women Beware Women* approvingly describes a Bianca whose "nervous excitement" when the Duke first sees her in the window carries into their physical encounter:

> The hint that Bianca is enamoured of the duke makes the
> rape scene especially ambiguous and this production did the

---

[90] Connolly, "In the Repertoire," 67; "it remains unclear," Connolly adds, "whether the issue of race as presented by the production added to an audience's sense of Bianca as anything more than a two-dimensional character."

[91] The image is included in Mentz, "*Women Beware Women*," 672, who also notes that the scene was staged as a seduction. The quotations are from an anonymous review at www.theatermania.com/news/women-beware-women_16594/.

play full justice in articulating the dangerous assumption that the duke's assault is in some way subliminally welcomed by Bianca. During the scene the duke stands behind her, entrapping her in his arms. The assault is brutal and revolting as he blames her beauty for the intransigence of his desire, but then as he places a hand on her breast and the other between her legs, her hand moves to meet and hold his. *We'll walk together*, says the duke, and, as he exits, she follows him still holding hands. Judy Damas's Bianca and Ian Barritt's duke succeeded in delineating the profoundly disturbing sexual politics of the scene without demystifying it – half rape, half seduction, but neither one nor the other.[92]

The idea that a woman might "subliminally welcome" a "brutal and revolting" assault is arguably a more dangerous assumption than any to be found in the original scene, and makes the sexual politics of such a performance more disturbing than the conventional rape-by-a-ruler that Middleton wrote. Even more than a staging that suggests Bianca's willingness from the outset, a rape that blurs into seduction because the assailant succeeds in provoking his victim's unacknowledged desire reproduces the myth that women secretly wish to be taken by force.

But if Bianca is raped by the Duke, and then does precisely the *opposite* of what a virtuous wife is supposed to do – she accepts her rapist's offer of wealth, power, and a continued sexual relationship – what is the play doing with this change to the traditional pattern? Critics who recognize the act as a rape tend also to see it as presenting some version of the other side of the conventional coin: a tainted body does indeed corrupt the soul, and Bianca's decision to survive her rape is the start of her moral deterioration, which culminates in her attempted murder of the Cardinal, her accidental poisoning of the Duke, and her own suicide, not for honor but from despair at having killed the man she has come to love. In *Women Beware Women*, observes Gossett, "rape is seen to lead inevitably to other crimes involving

---

[92] Smith, "*Women Beware Women*," 90. This review is cited by Connolly, "In the Repertoire," 67.

both victim and attacker." Noting that the play presents "Bianca's choice to end resistance and 'consent after' as morally corrupt but altogether reasonable," Detmer-Goebel claims that "*Women Beware Women* pessimistically envisions this power [of consent] as what endangers men's 'investment' in women's chastity." Carolyn D. Williams states the case most bluntly: "The necessity of speedy death [for a raped woman] is emphasized by the unseemly conduct of victims who persist in living," and Middleton thus offers Bianca up as "a carefully designed case study of moral degeneration."[93] I do not intend to mount a defense of Bianca's morality: there is very little morality to go around in Middleton's Florence, and Bianca is ruthless in her quest for self-preservation, even if her choices, arguably, are at least as constrained as they are corrupt. Should she submit to indefinite confinement in a hidey-hole at "the end of the dark parlour" (3.1.242), or abandon Leantio for the Duke? Should she report Leantio's death threats (4.1.81–88), or wait to see if he carries them out? Should she do away with the Cardinal, or live in fear of what he, as Florence's "next heir" (5.2.20), might do to his brother after he marries a woman the Cardinal abhors? I do think, though, that the play presents Bianca's survival in a way that questions the "virtuous" woman's prescribed trajectory of rape, pollution, shame, and death. Kahn observes that Bianca returns to the stage "fully aware that in the eyes of the world she is now a contaminated outcast . . . . Yet unlike Lucrece – paradigm of the raped wife – she does not take upon herself the indelible stain of rape."[94] Kahn develops this intriguing statement no further, as her essay's concerns are elsewhere, but in what follows I will argue that Bianca neither takes the stain upon herself nor

---

[93] Gossett, "Marrying the Rapist," 321; Detmer-Goebel, "Dramatizing Consent," 156; Williams, "Silence," 106. See also Bamford, *Sexual Violence*, p. 197 n.72, and Dawson, "Economy of Rape," 311–312. Hotz-Davies, "Feminism," 37, is a notable exception to the consensus, arguing instead that the play trivializes rape by showing it to leave no lasting traumatic effect. Regarding the rape's aftermath, I agree with Jowett's introduction to *Women Beware Women* in the *Collected Works*, p. 1490: Bianca "confronts an initially appalling prospect, after her fate and her identity have been decided for her, and . . . she adapts to it."

[94] Kahn, "New Directions," 167.

has it thrust upon her by the play. If the shame of rape is the shame of forced bodily pollution, then Bianca's response to her rape, in which first anger and then pragmatism predominates over shame, is affectively justified by the sheer disgust she expresses in the moments when she first returns to the stage, her body and mind newly flooded with the horror of forced intercourse: disgust that directs the audience's revulsion toward the *source* of the contamination rather than its unwilling object.

Before she turns defiantly on Guardiano, Bianca has seven lines of unguarded truth:

> Now bless me from a blasting! I saw that now
> Fearful for any woman's eye to look on.
> Infectious mists and mildews hang at's eyes,
> The weather of a doomsday dwells upon him.
> Yet since my honour's leprous, why should I
> Preserve that fair that caused the leprosy?
> Come, poison all at once! (2.2.420–423)

If an audience has any doubts about whether Bianca consented to the sex that has happened offstage, these lines should settle the matter: a consenting adulteress, seduced by venal temptations, does not normally emerge aghast from her first encounter to express revulsion at what she has experienced with her lover.[95] The reason for Bianca's revulsion – and indeed, the

---

[95] Surprisingly little attention has been paid to the trauma expressed in this passage as evidence of rape; to the best of my knowledge, only Hotz-Davies, "Feminism," 36 reads them as proof that the sex was nonconsensual. The rest of Bianca's speech, addressed to and condemning Guardiano, begins the anger that will define her character for the next several scenes. Her defiant self-comparison to a great man who "mak[es] politic use of a base villain" and "likes the treason well, but hates the traitor" is unlikely to be an honest admission that she enjoyed the encounter (why admit such a thing to the loathed Guardiano?), and is instead more of a piece with the aggressive self-possession with which she proceeds to treat everyone, from Livia to the Cardinal, who would seek to harm her. Bianca does not allow her enemies to see her pain.

revulsion itself – has been largely overlooked by literary critics, and while it should be obvious and constantly visible to a theater audience, it is often obscured in productions by casting decisions. Simply put, from Bianca's perspective, the Duke is an old man.[96] She is "about sixteen" (3.1.180); he is "about some fifty-five" (1.3.92). She is two or three years older than Shakespeare's Juliet; he is only five years younger than Chaucer's January, whose bristly face and flapping "slakke skin about his nekke" are regarded with such repugnance by his young bride ("The Merchant's Tale" 1824, 1849). A woman's revulsion at the prospect of sex with a much older man is a commonplace in early modern plays, from Fletcher's *The Tamer Tamed*, where Livia must evade marrying the elderly Moroso or face becoming "a dry-nurse to his coughs" (2.1.63), to Shakespeare's *The Merry Wives of Windsor*, where the wives inform Falstaff – "old, cold, withered, and of intolerable entrails" – that he couldn't possibly be their "delight" even if they *were* inclined to adultery (5.5.141, 144). As mentioned earlier, Menninghaus devotes a considerable amount of attention to the aged woman as the prototypical object of sexually inflected disgust:

> Almost all of the defects addressed and rejected by the discourse on disgust are repeatedly compressed into one single phantasm: that of the ugly old woman. This phantasm conventionally brings together folds and wrinkles, warts, larger than usual openings of the body (i.e. mouth and anus), foul, black teeth, sunk-in hollows instead of beautiful swellings, drooping breasts, stinking breath, revolting habits, and a proximity to both death and putrefaction.[97]

---

[96] On the age at which a man would be considered old, see Martin, *Constituting Old Age*, pp. 3–5, 13–14; among other sources proposing ages from forty to sixty, Martin cites Thomas Fortescue's placement of *senectus*, "our sixte age," as starting at fifty-five, followed only by the decrepit "seventh age" that begins at sixty-eight. Whether the Duke "is" old, however, is less relevant than the fact that a sixteen-year-old would find him so, particularly as a sexual partner.

[97] Menninghaus, *Disgust*, p. 84.

There is nothing here, drooping breasts included, that could not describe the aging *male* body; the disgusting sexualized body is gendered female, quite simply, because the authors of Menninghaus' sources, from antiquity onward, are male. Readers who turn to Bianca's first sight of the Duke from her window as evidence of her attraction to him are missing the irony of that passage.[98] The Mother, aged sixty (1.1.118), appropriately considers the Duke, five years her junior, a handsome man, although even she observes that he's attractive *for his age*: "a goodly gentleman of his years" (1.3.91). Bianca, having asked "Is he old, then?" and having been told his age, replies "That's no great age in man, he's then at best / For wisdom and for judgement" (1.3.93–94). Not only, of course, is Bianca about to find out just how far the Duke is from the kind of behavior that denotes wisdom and judgment, but her polite deflection of the Mother's remark about his good looks reveals what anyone who has ever been a sixteen-year-old girl already knows: wisdom and judgment, in the shape of men old enough to be their grandfathers, are not what teenaged girls find sexually attractive. Nothing Bianca says after she sees the Duke pass by in procession suggests she's changed her opinion: rather, she comments on the "reverence" – a word often associated with respect for age – of this "solemn and most worthy custom" (1.3.104–105). Bianca's recently awakened sexual appetite is directed toward her own young husband, who is likely in his mid to late twenties at most, the normal age at first marriage in early modern England for a man of his class; given the emphasis put on the imprudence of his elopement, Leantio may be even younger. Her physical desire for him is clearly conveyed in both her playful demands for kisses in the opening scene (1.1.142–148) and her later pleas that he delay his journey "But this one night" (1.3.49). Furthermore, whatever Leantio's faults may be, the play implies he is more than ordinarily good-looking, seeing that the experienced Livia conceives a violent passion for him at first sight. For a girl in her teens, whose first and only sexual experience has been with a beautiful, youthful, and actively desired male body, the decay of fifty-five – let alone

---

[98] See, for instance, Daalder, "State of the Art," 86–87, and Foster, "Deed's Creature," 511–512.

being forced into sexual contact with it – would indeed appear "Fearful for any woman's eye to look on."

The forty-year age difference between Bianca and the Duke, on top of the sheer unwantedness of what he does to her, is more than sufficient to explain the strong current of physical repulsion that permeates Bianca's moral coding of her experience – her feared damnation as "blasting," the reference to "doomsday," the figurative sickness of her "honour." Even as she observes her own contamination – imaging herself as healthy grain at risk of being "blasted" by the Duke's "mildews," and a patient newly infected with his "leprosy" – the audience hears first that what Bianca *saw* was revolting to her: "I saw that now / Fearful for any woman's eye to look on. / Infectious mists and mildews hang at's eyes, / The weather of a doomsday dwells upon him" (2.2.420–423). Mildew, which Gervase Markham describes as "a kind of filthy sooty blackness," is caused by "unwholesome air" – like the Duke's "infectious mists" – or by "over-ranknesse or to much fatnesse of the earth," and thus evokes the disgust associated with the uncontrolled fertility-in-decay of fungus, and with overripe excess more generally.[99] Another kind of early modern "mildew," also known as "honeydew," throws stickiness, unwholesome sweetness, and sheep-rot into the picture.[100] The statement that this filth "hangs at [the Duke's] eyes" makes one think irresistibly of eye discharge – due to rheumy age, infection, or both – no matter how metaphorical the image may be. That early moderns found eye discharge repugnant is confirmed, should such a thing require confirmation, by one of the epigrams in Robert Herrick's *Hesperides* that deliberately deploy disgust: "Seeal'd up with Night-gum, *Loach* each morning lies, / Till his Wife licking, so unglews his eyes."[101]

---

[99] Markham, *Markham's Farwell*, p. 97; Hagthorpe, *Divine Meditations*, p. 88. The information about "unwholesome air" is from Hagthorpe; the rest is from Markham.

[100] *OED* "mildew" n. 1. See also Fitzherbert, *Newe Tracte*, folio viiii v. In a section titled "What thynge rotteth shepe," Fitzherbert describes using one's tongue to detect a liquid "like hony" found in the morning on grass and leaves.

[101] Quoted in Eschenbaum, "Desiring Disgust," 60. Bromham, "Plague," 154, suggests the line about "infectious mists and mildews" implies the Duke is syphilitic.

Middleton himself has De Flores list "slimy" eyes, along with the wrinkles of age, as something that would make a man's face even more repellent than his own: "Wrinkles like troughs, where swine-deformity swills / The tears of perjury that lie there like wash / Fallen from the slimy and dishonest eye" (*The Changeling* 2.1.43–45). After the Duke's mildewed eyes, Bianca invokes the repulsive disfigurements of leprosy, a disease that not only caused hideous, elephantiasis-like growths and the eventual decay of the sufferer's facial features, but produced a foul stench.[102] It is most likely the leprosy itself that Bianca calls upon to "poison all at once," since poison, like leprosy, could be represented as eating away the flesh of its victim.[103] Bianca's lines, however, also call to mind the way in which leprosy was thought to spread: it was feared to be so contagious, and the body of the leper so extraordinarily contaminating, that those who suffered from the disease were subject to elaborate rules governing their contact with other people and with objects that others might touch; edicts against lepers going barefoot suggest a fear that they could contaminate even the ground itself.[104] When Bianca says "Yet since my honour's leprous, Why should I / Preserve that fair that caused the leprosy?" (2.2.421–422), the rape victim's conventional denunciation of her own beauty goes hand in hand with a reminder that what actually "causes" leprosy is very far from "fair": what causes leprosy is contact with the disgustingly disfigured body of someone who already has the disease. Once again, the play directs disgust back at the Duke, evoking Bianca's physical experience of him even as she laments her own early-stage infection – an infection that afflicts, we might note, only the abstraction that is her "honour"; in her formulation, it does not explicitly contaminate the material reality of her body. Livia, who at thirty-nine

---

[102] See Boeckl, *Images of Leprosy*; the horrifying disfigurements of leprosy are shown in photographs on pp. 11–13; the smell is mentioned on pp. 84–85, 89.

[103] On the corrosive effects of poison, see, for instance, *The Revenger's Tragedy* 3.5.159–161; 5.1.100–101.

[104] Boeckl, *Images of Leprosy*, pp. 38–39; Allen, *Wages of Sin*, pp. 36–37. The evidence in both texts is from the later Medieval period and includes other countries besides England; I have not found direct evidence of rules governing lepers in early modern England, but it seems safe to presume Middleton's audience would have been aware that leprosy was both loathsome and contagious.

prefers men far younger than fifty-five, aptly describes Bianca's reaction to sex with the Duke in terms of nausea, even as she dismisses it: "Her tender modesty is but seasick a little / .... / 'Tis but a qualm of honour; 'twill away" (2.2.470; 473).

For a modern audience to experience Bianca's disgust – not just to recognize how repulsed she is by forced sex with an old man, but to feel repulsed by it themselves – the visible age difference between Bianca and the Duke has to be marked enough to push past the Hollywood norms of mature leading men making onscreen love to much younger women, and tap into the quasi-physical repugnance felt for something like the sex crimes of Jeffrey Epstein: a man in late middle age preying on adolescent girls.[105] Early productions would have been far from evoking this effect: in 1962, the Royal Shakespeare Company (RSC) cast twenty-six-year-old Jeanne Hepple as Bianca; Geoffrey Chater, playing the Duke, was forty-one. Seven years later, the RSC staged the play again, with Judi Dench, aged thirty-four, as Bianca, and the Duke (Brewster Mason) a mere twelve years her senior.[106] Some more recent casting decisions, however, show an awareness of the possibilities offered by a play so unusually specific about the relative ages of its central characters. Marianne Elliott's 2010 production for the Royal National Theatre featured an age gap of about twenty-five years, and apparently played it up: Roberta Barker describes Lauren O'Neill's Bianca and Vanessa Kirby's Isabella as "painfully youthful lambs on their way to the inevitable slaughter," while a review by Philip Fisher calls the two characters "innocent 16 year olds . . . played by a pair of faces fresh to the London stage."[107] In this feminist staging of the play,

---

[105] My point is not that Middleton's original audience would have had anything akin to a modern conception of pedophilia, but that the appearance of a sixteen versus fifty-five age difference in a modern production can harness the audience's repugnance for that particular crime to produce a disgust-reaction consonant with the disgust the rape induces in Bianca.

[106] Casting details for these productions are found in Brown, "Professional Productions," 179–217; online searches provided the actors' dates of birth.

[107] Barker, "Freshly Creepy Reality," 135; Fisher, "*Women Beware Women*," www .britishtheatreguide.info/reviews/RNT-WBW-rev.htm.

which Barker praises for its "complex use of the tools of realist acting," Bianca was not only unambiguously raped but bore evidence of the "deep psychological wounds" of her assault through the rest of the play: through her abandonment of Leantio, in her scenes as the Duke's mistress, and up to the very end, "the actress continued to construct for Bianca the inner monologue of a traumatised survivor of sexual violation." The result was a production that "strove ... to render the fruits of a masculinist social order sickening rather than titillating."[108] Interestingly, a much earlier and far less feminist production – Howard Barker's notoriously problematic 1986 adaptation – seems also to have been aware of the "sickening" effect available to a director through the play's coupling of an underaged girl and a man of fifty-five, though that effect was used to very different ends. In Barker's *Women Beware Women*, where the first half of the script is Middleton's and the second his own creation, Bianca and the Duke emblematize an oppressive political order in which Bianca "allow[s] herself to be made a figurehead for a repressive government" and the Duke "assert[s] his divine right to rule by having what all men desire – money, power, sex – all made manifest through Bianca's body."[109] When Barker's play opened at the Royal Court, William Gaskill directed a cast that included twenty-five-year-old Joanne Whalley as Bianca and fifty-eight year old Nigel Davenport as the Duke. Costuming decisions stretched their thirty-three-year age difference disturbingly further: stills from the production show a white-haired, white-bearded Duke, while Bianca's hair is styled in girlish braids.[110] If disgust was indeed the intended effect, its object was the corrupt political system their pairing represented, not the act of rape itself; however,

[108] Barker, "Freshly Creepy Reality," 121, 135–136, 134. Richard Lintern, born 1962, played the Duke in this production; no birth date for O'Neill can be found online, but given her 2009 graduation from the Guildhall School of Music and Drama, she was most likely in her early twenties when she played Bianca.

[109] MacGregor, "Undoing the Body Politic," 20–21. MacGregor attempts to defend Barker's adaptation against charges of misogyny for rewriting the ending to include a second, "beneficial" rape of Bianca by Sordido; some of the charges are summarized by Connolly, "In The Repertoire," 64–66.

[110] Lechler, "Thomas Middleton," p. 55.

that Gaskill and Barker could harness the forty-year age gap of Middleton's original to this purpose speaks to the queasiness such a "couple" reliably generates, whether in Middleton's time, or Barker's, or our own.

The RSC's most recent production of *Women Beware Women*, directed by Laurence Boswell in 2006, not only observed Middleton's specified age difference but also evoked Bianca's disgust through an inspired bit of stage business. Stills available online show Hayley Atwell, aged twenty-three and looking like a teenaged Brooke Shields, playing Bianca opposite Tim Piggot-Smith, who was a few months away from his sixtieth birthday. The rape, which was very much a rape, was given extra visibility by its placement downstage rather than "above"; it was also "indicated symbolically by Pigott-Smith inserting his bejewelled finger into Bianca's mouth."[111] The stills show exactly how little Bianca wanted to be penetrated by that finger: Atwell's mouth is wide open, as if suffering a forced dental examination, and in one image, Pigott-Smith's finger appears thrust so far back in her throat as to risk a gag reflex.[112] In all likelihood, Atwell would have contended with her own disgust reaction each time she rehearsed or performed that scene; an audience watching an actor endure this fully real intrusion of another actor's bare hand into her mouth could not have avoided some vicarious sense of what she must be experiencing in the moment: the discomfort, the taste, the thought of sweat and germs. Thrusting a real finger into a real mouth stages more than a "symbolic" indication of how the Duke violates Bianca; within the limits of what one actor can do to another on an RSC stage, it powerfully transmits Bianca's reaction – the nauseated horror later indicated in the script – to forced intimate contact with the body of a much older man.

When Bianca's experience of rape is shown to leave her more disgust*ed* than disgust*ing*, it makes the conventional tropes of the sexually polluted woman that follow just a little harder to accept at face value. While the previous scene is still fresh in the audience's mind, Leantio comes home, smugly contemplating the fragrant cleanliness of marriage and the stinking filth of whores: marriage is like

---

[111] Connolly, "In the Repertoire," 70.
[112] See www.photostage.co.uk/drama/english-renaissance-drama/women-beware-women.html.

a banqueting house perfumed by a flower garden, where "the violet-bed's not sweeter" than the "delicious breath" of honest wedlock, but "base lust, / With all her powders, paintings, and best pride, / Is but a fair house built by a ditch side," and the "beautified body" of a strumpet is "a goodly temple / That's built on vaults where carcasses lie rotting" (3.1.88–89, 92–94, 98–99). Since the "ditch" is an open sewer, its smell wafting up into an unfortunately located house, Leantio here associates female sexual impurity with two prototypical objects of disgust: feces and putrescent flesh. On the surface, then, is the dramatic irony of a husband still ignorant of the fact that his chaste wife, in his absence, has been transformed into just such a reviled "strumpet"; but as these tropes come hard on the heels of the previous scene and the physical disgust it directs at the rapist, beneath the irony lies a sense that they are an uneasy fit for Bianca. The category of "polluted," as applied indiscriminately to all women defiled by nonmarital seed, with or without their volition, comes to appear facile, an unthinking assumption made by a man ignorant not only of what has happened to his wife, but of another thing the audience is keenly aware of: namely, of how it *felt* to her.

With this prelude to Bianca's career as the Duke's mistress, it is hard to see the play either as indicting her for failing to respond to her assault with the overwhelming shame that necessitates suicide, or as representing her trajectory as a cautionary tale of the inevitable moral deterioration of a woman who persists in living long enough to allow her rape-polluted body to cause the "decay" – to use Lucrece's word – of her soul. The scene of Leantio's homecoming offers only one, deeply ambiguous indication that Bianca may feel the traditional shame and bodily impurity of the rape victim: she repeatedly, insistently avoids his kiss, an explicit contrast to her pre-rape behavior that could signal a sense of herself as tainted, unworthy to receive marital affection and unable to do so without contaminating her yet-unwitting husband. However, it could also – or instead – signal her resignation to the fact that she is no longer Leantio's wife but the Duke's mistress, and/or her anger at Leantio for having left her to her fate, seeing that her last statement to him, before the Duke's messenger comes knocking, throws his departure in his face: "'Tis time to leave off dalliance; 'tis a doctrine / Of your own teaching, if you be remembered, / And I was bound to obey it" (3.1.168–170). Despite her ironic double-entendre about having had "the best content that Florence can afford," her unwillingness to kiss her husband seems unlikely to signal a sexual preference for the Duke, given both her initial reaction to intercourse with him, and the lack of any later indication of sexual desire or enjoyment on her part. To the extent that she comes to love him, it would seem to be more as a protector – between Leantio's threats and the Cardinal's, she certainly needs one – than as a sexual partner. In contrast to her early eagerness to kiss Leantio, her scripted kisses with the Duke, other than the suicidal one in the final scene, are explicitly at the Duke's request (3.2.236; 4.3.70). And, perhaps most tellingly, her one substantial soliloquy after she takes up residence at court is a wistful meditation on the vagaries of fate, in which she resolves that no daughter of hers will be subjected to the circumstances that led her, Bianca, to her present state (4.1.23–40). This speech is especially notable in that it directly follows an arch conversation with two court ladies in which they all compare lovers, after which one might reasonably expect Bianca's soliloquy to speak candidly of her own satisfaction, if not with her lover, then at least with her new life of luxury. But it offers no such insight, only the knowledge that she would not wish this life on her children.

What Bianca *does* want is the formal cementing of her protection, and the restoration of her own respectable status, two things achievable only through marriage to the Duke. And however deplorable both the Duke's logic and his methods in procuring this marriage might be – "Her husband dies tonight . . . . / Then I will make her lawfully my own, without this sin and horror" (4.1.270–273) – the play resists any suggestion that Bianca is too polluted to ever return to the status of chaste wife. Such a view is put in the mouth of the Cardinal, whose moral lectures to his brother have at their base the claim that to love a "fair strumpet" is to damn oneself for worthless filth: "Does the worm shun her grave? / If not – as your soul knows it – why should lust / Bring man to lasting pain for rotten dust?" (4.1.248–250). To the Cardinal, the woman who has had nonmarital sex is permanently, incurably tainted, impossible to cleanse by means of any subsequent marriage:

> Vowed you then never to keep strumpet more,
> And are you now so swift in your desires
> To knit your honours and your life fast to her?

> Is not sin sure enough to wretched man
> But he must bind himself in chains to't? Worse:
> Must marriage, that immaculate robe of honour
> That renders virtue glorious, fair, and fruitful
> To her great master, be now made the garment
> Of leprosy and foulness? Is this penitence
> To sanctify hot lust? What is it otherways
> Than worship done to devils? Is this the best
> Amends that sin can make after her riots
> As if a drunkard, to appease heaven's wrath
> Should offer up his surfeit for a sacrifice? (4.3.9–22)

Bianca, as the "strumpet" to whom the Duke's life and honor will be "knit," quickly becomes "sin" personified – if reducing her to an "it" can be termed personification – to which he will be "chained" by marriage; the remaining metaphors, of a foul, leprous body incongruously clothed in an "immaculate robe of honour," and a quantity of vomit offered up on an altar, thus are aimed at least as much at her, evoking the strumpet's conventional loathsomeness, as at any more abstract concept of the Duke's sinfulness. One does not even have to rely, though, on the usual untrustworthiness of cardinals in Jacobean tragedies (Middleton's audience were likely familiar with the ones in Webster's *The Duchess of Malfi* and *The White Devil*), to see that the Cardinal's unforgiving moral generalizations are those of a man who knows little, and perhaps cares even less, about how the woman he denigrates was lowered to her current status – a process the audience has witnessed in painful detail. Bianca's response, doctrinally correct in its implication that Christianity has no special, gendered category of indelible stain – "Heaven and angels / Take great delight in a converted sinner" (4.1.55–56) – evokes a common trope of the raped wife as a ruined temple. Lucrece's "sacred temple" is "spotted, spoiled, corrupted" (1172); Beaumont and Fletcher's Lucina demands whether Valentinian's "guilty eyes dare see these ruins / .... / The sacrilegious razing of this temple" (3.1.37–39); both feel the desecration to be irreparable. Bianca, however, concludes her plea for the Cardinal's charity with an assertion of the reparative value of marriage: "'Tis nothing virtue's temple to deface; /

But build the ruins, there's a work of grace" (4.3.68–69). In agreeing to become the Duke's mistress, Bianca has sinned; to have sinned is a cause for shame, but both sin and shame can be expunged through repentance. The shame of rape, as I have argued, is not the shame of knowing oneself to have committed a sin, but the shame of being polluted, helplessly disgusting to oneself and to others, and soiled in a way that repentance – what sin, after all, should a truly non-consenting victim repent? – cannot cleanse. In questioning this pollution itself, by directing the audience's visceral disgust at the rapist rather than at his victim, *Women Beware Women* thus questions the underpinnings of such shame, and the assumption that it is the natural and virtuous response to rape. To the extent that Bianca does *not* feel shame over what a disgusting old Duke saw fit to inflict on her, to the extent that she accepts her altered position afterward without internalizing conventional assumptions about a strumpet's supposedly indelible filth, she does indeed have a hope of being restored to her previous state.

Given that the play turns most of its major characters into murderers by the end and denies a happy ending to any of them, leaving only the Cardinal to moralize over the final bloodbath – one can imagine Florence's new duke with just the glimmer of a smile as he intones "So where lust reigns, that prince cannot reign long (5.2.225) – Bianca's end makes no statement on the physical pollution of rape causing a woman's moral degeneration. In her suicide, it is hard to separate her expressed love for the Duke – her final words celebrate the two of them "tasting the same death in a cup of love" (5.2.221) – from her entirely realistic fear of what will happen to her among Florence's courtiers now that her sole protector is dead, to be replaced as ruler by a man who abhors her: "What make I here? These are all strangers to me, / not known but by their malice, now th'art gone" (5.2.206–207). Bianca's suicide is not motivated by a belated sense of shame, nor enacted as a way to regain lost honor, either of which would undermine the play's questioning of the "virtuous" trajectory of rape, pollution, disgust, shame, and death. Instead, any sense that her death comes as punishment for her sins is balanced by the final scene's reminders of how Bianca came to be thrust into the wild corruption of the Florentine court and its hangers-on, and how little choice she had in the matter. Her last moments, even as she blames herself and the women who betrayed her, contain echoes of that speech of horror and disgust she gives directly following the rape: these include her literal death by poison, her suicidal kiss to suck the last breath from the Duke's "infected bosom," and her declaration that her "deformity in spirit's more foul; / A blemished face best fits a leprous soul" (5.2.192, 204–205).[113] Even her assailing of the Duke's unresponsive body, as she kisses his lifeless mouth – in search of death, not sexual gratification – offers an inverted reminder of the original encounter, in which he forced himself on her. There can be no happy ending for Bianca and the Duke, but only because theirs has never been a love story: Bianca's happiness, so evident in her opening scene with Leantio, comes to a violent end in an upstairs picture gallery. That her determination to live does not end with it – and to live not as a polluted strumpet, but as some respectable semblance of what she was before – is not, the play suggests, something of which she ought to be ashamed.

Titus Andronicus

The second and final play I will turn to is perhaps the most notorious for quite literally staging disgust. If the language of *The Rape of Lucrece* subtly performs disgust in a way that leads the reader to sympathize with the raped wife's intolerable shame, and *Women Beware Women* effectively turns the audience's disgust back on the rapist, the shockingly visible and visceral disgustingness of Shakespeare's *Titus Andronicus* questions the pollution-disgust-shame-suicide trajectory through a kind of double displacement of disgust: first from the invisible to the visible, and next from the victim to the perpetrators. Like Bianca in *Women Beware Women*, Lavinia survives her rape: she does not succumb to her horrific injuries, nor does she take her own life. Her choice to go on living would seem to be just that: a choice. Despite her rapists' taunts about her lacking the hands she needs to hang herself, the play never implies she is physically incapable of suicide: as several critics have noted, Marcus explicitly mentions a method that has been available to Lavinia all along when he offers that he and Lucius could "all headlong hurl [themselves]" from a high place, "And on the ragged

---

[113] Roma Gill's footnote to these lines draws the connection to the rape scene. See Gill, ed., *Women Beware Women*, p. 111.

stones beat forth [their] souls" (5.3.131–132).[114] The terms of Lavinia's survival, however, could not be less like Bianca's, as her rape is not a casual expression of lust and power with a consolation prize attached, but lust harnessed to an act of revenge, with the goal of inflicting maximum, permanent suffering. Lavinia's reasons for refusing the Lucrece model of rape's aftermath are also more inscrutable than Bianca's: her sole act of direct communication after the rape is to take her late sister-in-law's copy of Ovid's *Metamorphoses*, turn to the tale of Philomela, and then use her mouth and stumps to guide a stick in the sand and write *Stuprum – Chiron – Demetrius*. Even then, however, even once she has disclosed the crime and its perpetrators, Lavinia persists in living, in defiance of the tradition that demands she cleanse the stain of rape with her own blood after entrusting revenge to her male kin.

What I want to argue here is that *Titus Andronicus* works with disgust in a way that challenges its audience to question whether the rape victim's involuntary pollution can only be removed by her death. Through generating and harnessing its audience's disgust, the play experiments with the possibility of a revenge for rape that feels so fitting and so complete that it obviates the need for further purification. If, as with Shakespeare's Lucrece, Lavinia's so-called shame is intrinsically tied up in her transformation into an object of disgust, then by the logic of revenge – and quite *unlike* Lucrece – she can return her shame to her attackers by transforming them into something even more vile. In her illuminating exploration of revenge as a form of trauma therapy in *Titus*, Deborah Willis puts it this way: "In the language of revenge, quitting a wrong often involves returning it, preferably in the 'throat' of the wrongdoer (1.1.554; 3.1.275). When a debt has been quitted (i.e., repaid), it ceases to exist. When something is 'returned,' one no longer has it. It is as if the wrong, along with the suffering it produced, could be transformed into an object and 'returned to sender,' like an unwanted present."[115] Like Willis's, my analysis is concerned with the affective dimension of revenge: not whether baking Goths in pies

---

[114] See, for instance, Aebischer, "Women Filming Rape," 141; Williams, "Silence," 107; Howard, "Interrupting," 662.

[115] Deborah Willis, "Gnawing Vulture," 33.

actually solves any of Rome's problems, but whether, on the irrational, visceral level at which contamination-disgust toward the raped woman works anyway, such an act can remove the victim's stain. The rapist's blood, spilled in revenge as is traditional to the Lucrece narrative and its early modern descendants such as *Valentinian* or *The Revenger's Tragedy*, does nothing to de-contaminate his victim. The rapist's flesh, as we will see, may be a different story.

As Willis observes, feminist analyses of *Titus Andronicus* have "tended to downplay women's participation in revenge, emphasizing instead their role as victim," a tendency particularly pronounced in the case of Lavinia, whose role in the Andronici's revenge plot is "either ignored or viewed as imposed on her." In such analyses, the male members of her family are "represented as reducing Lavinia to an object, silencing her, or subjecting her to a patriarchal script."[116] Oddly enough, given her critique of this tradition, Willis also eventually shies away from exploring the full implications of Lavinia as an active revenger. After a brilliant examination of the "theater of revenge" that Tamora stages in order to "reclaim. . . dominance through enacting a fantasy of undoing the past through reversal, [and] purging her own feelings of humiliation and powerlessness by projecting them onto Titus," the argument about Lavinia then minimizes the extent of her role in avenging her own rape:

> What is it, then, that Lavinia "says" to her father in these scenes? Using gestures, a copy of Ovid's *Metamorphoses*, and her uncle's staff, she finds a way to express her pain and grief, to describe what happened to her in the forest, and eventually to name those who raped and maimed her (4.1.1–78). She enters into a pact with her male relatives to seek "mortal revenge" upon her enemies (ll. 87–94) . . . . [Titus'] struggle to "interpret all her martyr'd signs (3.2.36) comes to settle on deciphering the names of those who raped and maimed her, and he presses her into service as an assistant in the project of revenge. Yet even here it is Lavinia who

116   Ibid., 22.

initiates the discovery of her rapists' names by chasing young Lucius and making frantic gestures over the school-boy text of Ovid's *Metamorphoses*. Perhaps it is more accurate to say that Titus has offered and Lavinia has accepted revenge as a strategy for coping with grief and shame.[117]

It is, I would argue, even more accurate to say that in act four, scene one, *Lavinia* is the one to offer the revenge strategy and Titus accepts it. What Lavinia shows the Andronici in that copy of Ovid is, of course, the story of Philomela. Lavinia, unlike Philomela, has no sister to aid her in her revenge, but she once had a sister-in-law, and it is surely no coincidence that this, we are told, was her book; we further learn that the two women had been close, given that Marcus speculates, half-correctly, that Lavinia has chosen the book "For love of her that's gone" (4.1.43). Aided, however indirectly, by Procne's substitute, Lavinia's one clear and autonomous instance of communication after her rape and mutilation is to identify herself with Philomela, a move that not only clarifies the crime committed against her, but makes two important declarations: first, her desired mode of revenge, and second, her rejection of death as the end to her story. Feminist readings that stress Titus's male appropriation of Procne's revenge and Lavinia's disempowerment in lacking the female community of a sister thus seem to me to deny Lavinia the one bit of agency the play grants her – the agency she seizes along with that copy of *The Metamorphoses* and enacts when she holds the basin between her stumps to "receive the blood."[118] Where Titus betrays his daughter and re-animates the patriarchal rape-as-shame script is not in failing to collaborate with her to obtain the revenge she desires, but in suddenly and unexpectedly refusing to let her see it through to its full Ovidian conclusion, in which Philomela herself partici-pates in revealing the main ingredient of Tereus' dinner, and does *not* die:

[117] Ibid., 40–41, 43, 48.

[118] See, for instance, Kahn, *Roman Shakespeare*," pp. 62–65; Robertson, "Appropriation," 218–220, 228–229; Sale, "Representing Lavinia," 18–21; Brockman, "Trauma and Abandoned Testimony," 358–361; Detmer-Goebel, "Lavinia's Voice," 86–88.

her transformation into a nightingale is neither Lucrece's choice of suicide over shame, nor Virginia's consent (the precedent Titus invokes when he kills Lavinia) to her sacrifice at the hands of her father.[119]

While much work has been done on *Titus Andronicus*'s adaptation of the Philomela myth, Ovidian readings of Lavinia have a tendency to take the play's treatment of both parts of the myth – Philomela's cannibal revenge, and her final transformation – and make them fit the same critical narrative: most commonly a narrative of Lavinia's disempowerment, although a few take the opposite position. Critics who see Titus' fifth-act slaying of his daughter as a murder, an unwarranted patriarchal deviation from Ovid to Livy (i.e., to the stories of Lucrece and Virginia), tend to read Lavinia's role in the slaughter of Chiron and Demetrius as obedience to patriarchal authority. Carolyn Sale, for instance, calls Lavinia's death an "execution" and astutely observes that Titus "opts for the Lucretian narrative of rape over the Ovidian one" when he makes his daughter "pay the price for the discourse of shame within which he situates her body"; yet Sale's essay elides Lavinia's revenge by focusing on the story of Philomela as "*amongst other things*, a tale about the effective and powerful transmission of a text between women" (my italics). Surely, those "other things" are also very much to the point, but Sale's only reference to the slaughter of Chiron and Demetrius reads it, too, as a patriarchal imposition: Titus "asserts Lavinia's status as an involuntary receptacle for the fluids of men by making her hold up the bowl into which [their] blood pours from their slit necks."[120] Conversely, Christian Billing sees the Philomela myth as indicating the revenge that Lavinia desires and actively achieves; however, he then extends it to authorize her death as well: "the intertextual frame of reference. . .powerfully foreshadows the female vengeance that is to come and highlights not only Lavinia's role in the capture and mutilation of Chiron and Demetrius but her eventual corporeal release from the torment of physical and emotional suffering."[121] To my knowledge, only Pascale

---

[119] On the Philomela myth as an empowering "countertradition" to Lucrece, see Newman, "Mild Women," 305.

[120] Sale, "Representing Lavinia," 20–21.

[121] Billing, "Cutting Ovid's Tongue," 68.

Aebischer has recognized that Lavinia's identification with the Philomela myth indicates *both* facets of what she wants: first, "the recipe for the Andronici's revenge," and then her own continued survival, adhering to the precedent of the woman who "lives on in the shape of a nightingale, thus acquiring a new voice."[122] "What never ceases to amaze me about Lavinia's death," writes Aebischer, "is the sheer endorsement Titus receives from critics and performers alike for his wresting of her into another myth which prescribes her destruction. It is as if everybody was secretly relieved to be rid of the obscenity her mangled body forces on us, as if there existed a conspiracy to refigure murder as euthanasia or assisted suicide."[123] Starting from this recognition, and considering how the dynamics of disgust might work in *Titus Andronicus*, we can begin to see how Lavinia's revenge is so far from arbitrary or merely imitative that it might actually take her shame and pollution and, in Willis's terms, truly return them to sender: "Once something is 'returned,' one no longer has it."[124] If Lavinia no longer has what Chiron and Demetrius "gave" her, then she *can*, to give Saturninus' words a meaning he does not intend, "outlive her shame," and an early modern audience may well be swayed to feel that she has effectively done so. That her father thinks otherwise turns out to be the culminating horror of Lavinia's ordeal.

To understand how shame intersects with disgust in the rape scenario of *Titus Andronicus*, a brief comparison with *The Rape of Lucrece* is useful. As we have seen, Lucrece states her own feelings of shame explicitly and at length, while the idea that the rape has made her physically disgusting – defiled and soiled in a way that is largely unrelated to guilt or blame – functions as a kind of subtextual affective justification for a shame that is morally unjustified. Lucrece, immediately following the rape, becomes

---

[122] Aebischer, "Women Filming," 41; Aebischer, "Silencing," 32.
[123] Aebsicher, "Silencing," 33. See also Packard, "Lavinia as Coauthor," 295. Packard, who allows for both Lavinia's initiative in identifying with Philomela and her active participation in the revenge, observes that "Titus's murder of Lavinia is a belated enactment of the sacrifice narrative" but offers no detailed analysis of the revenge itself.
[124] Willis, "Gnawing Vulture," 33.

Tarquin's "surfeit" (698–700) and even his "vomit" (703–704) as well as the polluted receptacle of the revoltingly literal "load of lust he leaves behind" (734). In *Titus Andronicus*, the shame/disgust dynamic works differently. Partly because her mutilations have impaired her ability to communicate, there is very little evidence that what Lavinia feels after her rape is shame. Shame is certainly implied in her plea to Tamora, where her desire to protect even her dead body from exposure to the male gaze is evident when she begs to be spared from the brothers' "worse-than-killing lust" and instead killed and "tumbled" in a pit "where never man's eye may behold [her] body" (2.3.175–177). Following the rape, shame is also read briefly onto the brutalized, bloodied Lavinia by Marcus, who interprets her reaction to his guess that "some Tereus hath deflowered [her]" as her averting her face "for shame" and blushing, although a blush, as even he acknowledges, is unlikely in someone suffering from "all this loss of blood" (2.3.26–32). Here, though, the improbability of Lavinia's blush may well cast doubt on Marcus's assumption about her shame, opening the possibility for a staging that defies it. Such was Thomas Oldham's sense of the scene in the 2014 Globe revival of Lucy Bailey's *Titus*, with Flora Spencer-Longhurst as Lavinia: "Despite Marcus's line, which necessitates the director blocking the actor so that she turns away, the affective impression I received was not one of humiliation or embarrassment. Spencer-Longhurst's face conveyed much, including frustration at the inability to speak, but the affect that came through most powerfully was one of suffering. After briefly averting her gaze, she returned it powerfully back on Marcus, eyes bulging in a display of agony. . . . That is what I felt in her turning away, not shame."[125] Finally, of course, there are Titus' last words to his daughter, to which I will return in due course: "Die, die, Lavinia, and thy shame with thee / And with thy shame thy father's sorrow die" (5.3.45). These are the only two moments in the play where other characters explicitly attribute shame to Lavinia, and of the two, only Marcus's (highly unreliable) lines refer primarily to Lavinia's affective state rather than to her dishonored status. In the many passages where the men "interpret" her, their interpretations do not revolve around the theme of shame in the way

[125] Oldham, "Affective Appeal," 82.

we might expect them to. It would be all too easy for interpretations like Marcus's to be repeated to the point that they determine the audience's "knowledge" of Lavinia's interiority, but this does not happen. Moreover, as Titus' famous laughter at the return of his severed hand and his sons' heads should remind us, this is not a play in which characters always have the expected affective response.[126] So what *can* we know about what Lavinia feels? Mute and handless, reliant on Ovid's text for most of what she communicates, she produces only a single word of her own to describe what has been done to her: *stuprum*. *Stuprum*, as we learn in Diana C. Moses' examination of the concept's history, stressed not the forcible nature of a sexual act, but the idea that one person had been passively and shamefully "used" by another to satisfy the active party's lust: "The archaic notion of *stuprum* seems to have been one of pollution, so that the victim, however innocent of causing the act, was nevertheless irreparably tainted."[127] For anyone who has seen a production of *Titus* and has been unable to get the image out of their head of act two, scene four's horrifically mutilated, unbandaged, suffering Lavinia, bones poking through her chopped wrists and blood pouring from the stump of her tongue, Lavinia's self-declared sense of her own injuries – *stuprum*, defilement, pollution, uncleanness – melds with the audience's experience of a sight liable to induce the involuntary visceral recoil that is disgust. We barely need Gail Kern Paster's reminder that Lavinia's bleeding mouth represents her violated genitals, nor the hints in *Lucrece* about seminal "loads of lust" to see and feel that what Lavinia's rapists have done to her, inside and out, is to have made her disgusting.[128]

---

[126] As Willis, "Gnawing Vulture," 34, observes, *Titus* subjects the audience to a similar affective experience: "This is a play that at times evokes bizarrely inappropriate emotions and disjunction between thoughts and feeling."

[127] Moses, "Livy's Lucretia," 49. Detmer-Goebel, "Lavinia's Voice," 86, observes that the word, which is not used in Ovid's tale of Philomela, indicates "uncleanliness" and names Lavinia's transformed state as well as what was done to her.

[128] Paster, *The Body Embarrassed*, pp. 98–99.

Modern directors, actors, and audience members are no strangers to how Lavinia's appearance *with her hands cut off, her tongue cut out, and ravished*, produces revulsion. Rose Reynolds, who played Lavinia in Michael Fentiman's 2013 RSC production, described what the scene can do to an audience: "Lavinia's entrance after her rape and mutilation is notorious for causing audience members to experience extreme reactions; this was notable in Lucy Bailey's production at the Globe in 2006. In our production we have had people have to leave, vomit, or faint and I'm told there are sick bags at the end of each row." Reynolds herself not only carried a blood bag in her mouth to burst at the appropriate moment, but chewed licorice blackjacks to blacken her tongue, producing the illusion of a gaping wound in a realistically tongueless mouth.[129] A colleague of mine who led a group of undergraduates on a field trip to Bailey's *Titus* recalls that one of her students threw up when Lavinia's raw stumps squirted blood in a realistic simulation of severed arteries, and another felt so close to passing out that she fled the theater. Reviewers used words like "stomach-churning" for this particular scene; one reported that fifteen audience members had been carried out during the show she attended.[130] Even a more stylized approach to Lavinia's injuries, like Yukio Ninagawa's in 2006, which used streaming clumps of red wool in place of stage blood, can evoke similar revulsion: Billing's review described the wool-festooned amputations as "not only deeply disturbing in their suggestion of blood but also in their evocation of limbs that ha[d] been violently ripped from their sockets, pulling with them an assortment of veins, muscles and sinews."[131] A more naturalistic Lavinia, as played by Jennifer Woodburne in a 1995 production in Johannesburg, added a bodily fluid that continued to flow after the blood had been stanched: she had researched wound management for her role and observed a man with a tongue amputation, whose saliva poured continually from his

---

[129] Dixon, "Violence"; Dickson, "Gory Details." The audience's affective experience of Bailey's 2006 *Titus* is analyzed extensively by Oldham, "Affective Appeal"; Whipday, "My tears," discusses how several recent productions, including Bailey's (2006 and 2014), stage Lavinia's suffering in ways that engage with current cultural conversations about violence against women.

[130] Friedman, *Titus*, p. 268.   [131] Quoted in Friedman, *Titus*, p. 236.

mouth because of his trouble swallowing. In an interview, Woodburne said, "I thought, what would it be like for Lavinia, who had been this, like *princess* in Rome. . . what would it be like for her to have saliva running out of her mouth all the time and no hands to wipe it away?"[132] The beginning of Marcus's infamously poetic speech detailing his niece's injuries arguably heightens the disgust effect through its incongruous eroticization of her mutilated arms, "whose circling shadows kings have sought to sleep in" (2.4.19) and bleeding mouth, with its "roséd lips" (2.4.24) and "honey breath" (2.4.25): it is stomach-churning enough to *see* Lavinia in this state, without being induced to imagine touching, kissing, and smelling her as well. If the raped Lucrece is presented as just polluted enough to be sexually titillating, the eroticization of the horrifically, visibly defiled Lavinia, as Cynthia Marshall observes, takes *Titus* into the realm of hardcore fetish pornography: for most viewers, the effect is that of "a pornographic image that destroys eroticism by showing too much."[133] As in comparable kinds of modern fetish pornography, what fails to arouse frequently has the ability to revolt.

That Lavinia's mutilations are liable to evoke an affect that onlookers will register as disgust is borne out by a recent psychological study titled "Why are injuries disgusting? Comparing Pathogen Avoidance and Empathy Accounts," which found that the feeling evoked by viewing horrifically painful injuries (e.g., "seeing someone's bone sticking out of their leg") is not in fact "produced by the same psychological mechanism" as the feeling evoked by encountering things – like a hand covered in warts, or a cockroach – that could potentially make one ill. Despite scientifically measurable differences between the two reactions, however, the study found that

---

[132] Quoted in Tempera, "Staging the Mutilated Roman Body," 114.

[133] Marshall, *Shattering*, pp. 109–110, 130–131, 127. See also Aebischer, *Shakespeare's Violated Bodies*, p. 51; Aebischer describes Lavinia's horrifying post-rape entrance in Xavier Leret's 2001 *Titus*, when Jane Hartley turned to face the audience in a ripped skirt that exposed her bloodied crotch, making it "no longer possible to dissociate the violation of the character from that of the actor." Audience members were heard gagging through the scene that followed.

> When an injury is seen, it is empathically simulated and
> vicariously felt by the observer. Vicarious pain and harm is
> unpleasant to experience, so the observer wants to look
> away from the stimulus. The feeling is subjectively similar
> to disgust, and because a more precise term is lacking in the
> English lexicon, people use the closest term available to
> them and label the feeling as *disgust*.[134]

Furthermore, the study demonstrated that "the level of disgust reported
toward injury images was predominantly explained by how painful and
horrific the injury was perceived to be, rather than by how infectious and
contaminating it was perceived to be," a finding "consistent with the
hypothesis that the predominant emotional response toward injuries is
vicarious pain and horror, and these feelings are nevertheless interpreted
as disgust. . . . In other words, the more painful and horrific participants
found an injury to be, the more disgusting they reported it to be."[135]
Empathy with Lavinia is thus not remotely at odds with disgust at her
sickening physical condition; rather, in this context, empathy and disgust go
hand in hand – and a male audience member who might find it difficult to
vicariously feel the horrifying vaginal injury of a gang rape (an injury,
moreover, that is not visible on stage) has the same vulnerable hands and
tongue as any woman. In a 2015 production by the Smooth Faced
Gentlemen, an all-female company, the injury-disgust quotient was upped
by the addition of "an onstage, wordless interlude, during which [the
audience witnessed] the amputation of Lavinia's hands (using a stage effect
involving a bucket)."[136] What the play does, then, is to take the conventional assumption that Lavinia's condition is shameful – that she herself, in
the tradition of early modern and classical rape victims, suffers primarily
from shame and is viewed by others as shamed – and subsume the shame of
rape in its graphic depiction of how rape's pollution of its victim works in an
extraordinarily material way, producing the kind of visibly violated body
that evokes the visceral recoil of disgust.

---

[134] Kupfer, "Injuries," 961, 959–960.   [135] Ibid., 966.
[136] Whipday, "My tears," 265.

In fact, the sheer, obtrusive visibility of Lavinia's mutilations in performance may itself work to overwhelm the contamination-disgust typically directed toward the rape victim, along with its concomitant sense that to be contaminated – to be infected and defiled with the filth of nonmarital semen – is inherently shameful. The audience "knows" that Lavinia, within the fiction, has been contaminated with Goth semen, just as the reader knows that Lucrece has been contaminated with Tarquin's, but in *Titus* this knowledge of a fictional truth is at a remove from the blood, bones, raw or bandaged stumps, and whatever else is very materially *there* with the actor's body on stage. The audience knows the actor playing Lavinia has not been raped; but while the audience also knows that the actor's hands and tongue are safely intact, the visceral reaction to visible injuries and blood, as numerous fainting and vomiting spectators have demonstrated, is not mitigated by the knowledge that one is looking at prosthetic bones, an artificially blackened tongue, and a harmless liquid made of "mainly sugar and ice-cream colouring."[137] The post-rape Lavinia has been rendered *so* disgusting that the horror of viewing her amputations, as simulated on a real body in performance, may well obliterate the shame-producing aspect of her condition – the specifically sexual pollution with nonmarital semen – in a wave of excruciating, vicarious disgust-empathy.

Once shame has been subsumed into disgust, Lavinia can, in the logic of revenge, rid herself of it by "returning" it to Chiron and Demetrius. The gendered cultural valuation of chastity, of course, normally ensures that the rape victim's violation is similarly gendered, in a way that prevents it from being reciprocated onto a male body: in other words, the Andronici could order a painful, humiliating, retaliatory rape of Chiron and Demetrius, but they could not make it *mean* precisely the same thing. Some violations, however, are equal opportunity: there are ways to make a male body just as disgusting as a female body, and using that body to violate the most fundamental of Western food taboos is about as far as one can go in doing so.[138] Writing on *The Bloody Banquet*, a 1609 tragedy by Middleton and Dekker in which an adulterous queen is forced to dine, with full

---

[137] Dickson, "Gory Details."

[138] On the horror of cannibalism as ungendered, see Taylor, "Gender, Hunger," 22.

awareness, on her lover's corpse, Gary Taylor observes that cannibalism, in the early modern theater and the aptly termed modern genre of *cinéma vomitif* alike, presents us with the monstrosity not only of the eater, but of the eaten. Monsters, "the defining feature of horror films," are monstrous through their mixing of categories: "In particular, the monster is partly human and partly not. . . . The cannibal is a monster, because he or she is human, but he or she is also an animal, who like other nonhuman animal predators preys upon humans. In doing so, cannibals turn their victims into something monstrous too: a human is who also simultaneously an animal, like the other animals whose carcasses we butcher and eat." So strong is the taboo against cannibalism that a human carcass prepared for consumption is liable to produce "instantaneous visceral revulsion," revulsion that is all the stronger when the carcass is *seen*, as it would be on stage: "typically, seeing produces a stronger and less controllable reaction than reading. Reading is a learned cultural process, intellectually mediated; seeing, by contrast, is a biological animal function, and thus more directly wired to physical responses like nausea."[139] When Lavinia takes her late sister-in-law's copy of Ovid, turns to the tale of Philomela, and writes "*Stuprum–Chiron–Demetrius*" in the sand, she knows what's served up at the end of that story. In fact, given the connotations of *using* another's body that attach specifically to *stuprum*, as opposed to the English "rape," one might justifiably suspect that "*Stuprum–Chiron–Demetrius*" is meant to go both ways: *stuprum* is what her attackers did to her; *stuprum* is what she wants done to her attackers. What more definitive way could there be to "use" a male body for one's own gratification than to use it for meat?

At this point someone might object that while human meat is disgusting – it is disgusting to see it and disgusting to think about eating it – the disgust it causes does not attach to the now-deceased individual from whom it was taken. Julie Taymor's film version of *Titus*, for instance, clearly intends the viewer to be revolted by the sight of the big, juicy slabs of pie with their

---

[139] Ibid., pp. 28, 27. The term "*cinéma vomitif*" is from Brottman, *Offensive Films*, cited in Taylor, "Gender, Hunger," 24. Cannibalism and the revulsion it provokes are historicized in two very different contexts by Goldstein, *Eating and Ethics*, pp. 32–66, and Noble, *Medical Cannibalism*, pp. 35–57.

filling of slightly bloody ground meat that Titus serves at the banquet, but it would be difficult to argue that this pie produces physical disgust at Chiron and Demetrius *as* Chiron and Demetrius, a physical revulsion that goes beyond the "moral disgust" – their actions, after all, fit most definitions of that problematic category – that the audience is likely to have felt toward them for most of the play. The trouble with Taymor's pies, however, is that she doesn't follow Shakespeare's recipe: what the playtext indicates is in fact a pie that produces physical revulsion at Chiron and Demetrius *as themselves*. While, from a culinary perspective, Titus' threatened pie crust made of powdered bone for flour and blood for water is probably impracticable, it seems entirely likely that the filling is exactly as he states. He will make, he says, "two pasties of [their] shameful heads" (5.2.189), shortly afterward repeating "and in that paste let their vile heads be baked" (5.2.200). These heads are not only the precise payback of revenge for Titus having been returned the heads of his own decapitated sons, but a crucial feature of Philomela's vengeance as well.[140] While Procne takes the main role in seizing and killing her son Itys – Philomela's part, in Golding's translation, is a single, terse line, "The t'other sister slit / His throat" – and both sisters share the cooking, Itys' head is what provides Philomela with her climactic moment of revelation and triumph. After Tereus has consumed his meal,

> . . . out
> Lept Philomel with scattered haire aflight, like one that fled
> Had from some fray where slaughter was, and threw the bloody head
> Of Itys in his father's face. And never more was she
> Desirous to have had her speech that able she might be
> Her inward joy with worthy words to witness frank and free.[141]

---

[140] Willis, "Gnawing Vulture," 49, makes the point that Titus's specific reference to "heads" here recalls his sons' decapitation; to my knowledge, no critic to date has linked these heads to Philomela's use of Itys's.

[141] Forey, ed. *Ovid's Metamorphoses*, p. 198.

Two "vile heads" that are recognizable as those of Chiron and Demetrius, despite being severed and baked, are surely what are displayed, in all their staring, possibly hairy, intact repulsiveness, to the assembled company when Saturninus says "go fetch them hither to us presently" and Titus declares "why, there they are, both baked in this pie" (5.3.58–59). A head in a pie, moreover, would have been close enough to actual culinary practice for an early modern audience to increase the disgust value of a *human* head in a pie: the recipe for "a Hare pie" in Gervase Markham's *Countrey Contentments*, or *The English Huswife* (1623) instructs the cook to "reserve the head" before she parboils the meat, and then continues: "having raysed the coffin long-wise to the proportion of a *Hare*, first, lay in the head, and then the aforesaid meate, and lay the meate in the true portion of a *Hare*, with necke, shoulders, and leggs, and then cover the coffin and bake it as other bak't meates of that nature."[142] While it would be highly unlikely for Chiron and Demetrius to have appeared baked in their "true portion" in the play's original productions – a shape likely to raise suspicion, aside from other practical problems – various kinds of stagecraft could easily be employed to reveal their heads, from the false heads made of wax, paint, and (sometimes) animal entrails commonly used on the early modern stage, to simply having the actors, in appropriately revolting makeup, crouch under a draped table with their heads visible in the cut pie above.[143] A few modern directors have followed the textual cues: Ninagawa had a cart bearing two pies wheeled to center stage during the confusion in the moments after Lavina's death, whereupon "the faces of Chiron and Demetrius became grotesquely visible to the audience within the pies, which dripped strands of red wool"; in Blanche Mcintyre's 2017 RSC production, Titus pulled the sons' "flaccid, disintegrating faces" out of the pie to display to Tamora as she retched over the table; Silviu Purcarete's Romanian-language *Titus*, which toured from 1992 to 1997, had Titus reveal the heads from beneath domed silver dish-covers, slice off

---

[142] Markham, *Countrey Contentments*, p. 99.

[143] See Kenny, "Staging Dismemberment," 91. A production of *Titus* needs a pair of severed heads for act 3, scene 1, so these props could be made up as Chiron and Demetrius after serving as the heads of Titus's sons.

a bit of ear, taste it, and then force-feed it to Tamora, who "sat with it in her open mouth, paralysed by the sight of her sons' severed heads on the table in front of her."[144] Whether revealed, early modern hare style, as a pie's defining ingredient, or modernized for the shock value of a human head served up like a deluxe entrée, Chiron and Demetrius are supposed to be recognizably themselves in their cooked state: themselves rendered unspeakably, stomach-churningly disgusting.

This revelation should be the culminating moment of Lavinia's revenge, the play's equivalent of the moment when Philomela flings Itys' head at the man who raped her: the moment that *gets rid of* what has been inflicted on her – namely, disgustingness – by returning it, magnified, to those who inflicted it. But directly before this climax of disgust, Titus reverts to talking about Lavinia's "shame." Shame is a word and a concept that the play has not associated with Lavinia since Marcus's speech in Act 2, yet now, just before Lavinia's chosen Ovidian narrative reaches its triumphant conclusion, Titus invokes Virginius, prompts Saturninus to approve that a daughter "enforced, stained, and deflowered" should be killed so as not to "survive her shame," and declares "Die, die, Lavinia, and thy shame with thee / And with thy shame thy father's sorrow die" (5.3.38–40, 45–46). What Sale has called "the Lucretian narrative's construction of the violated female body as the text of the woman's shame, a text which can be expunged only by destroying the medium upon which it is written" returns unexpectedly, incongruously, and in a form where "shame" becomes visible not as the affective experience of the rape victim – the affect visible *as* affect here, if any, is that of the speaker, Titus's sorrow – but as what we might call the cultural position that rape confers on a woman and her male kin.[145] By having Titus invoke Lavinia's so-called shame and unexpectedly kill her for it seconds before her chosen disgust-based revenge reaches its full completion, the play snatches away the satisfaction it has built its audience up to expect, and for at least a moment, before full-on mayhem breaks out, makes

---

[144] Ninagawa and Purcarete are mentioned in Friedman and Dessen, *Titus*, pp. 239, 171–172; Mcintyre's handling of the pie scene is noted in Mills, "Review: *Titus Andronicus*."

[145] Sale, "Representing Lavinia," 21.

the traditional purificatory death of the raped woman *feel* like the unfair patriarchal imposition that it is.

In their history of modern productions of *Titus Andronicus* up to 2007, Michael Friedman and Alan Dessen record Lavinias who actively welcome their own deaths at Titus' hand, Lavinias who obediently submit to it, catatonic Lavinias so damaged as to be without visible volition by the time Titus lovingly euthanizes them, and even a pacifist Lavinia so horrified by Titus' gruesome revenge on her rapists that he finally dispatches her to prevent her from disrupting his plans.[146] The final Lavinia whose performance makes it into the book – played by Colleen Delany in Gale Edwards' 2007 production with the Shakespeare Theater Company in Washington, DC – was an exceptionally tough and resilient character, who single-mindedly sought revenge against her rapists, participated in their slaughter with glee, and raised her bandaged stumps in triumph as their bodies were carried off stage. And yet she too "willingly offered herself up for death," a choice Edwards justified as Lavinia being "corrupted and crushed" by her devotion to vengeance, and losing her will to live once she had achieved her goal.[147] Emma Whipday's analysis of Lavinias in productions between 2006 and 2017 notes a certain ambiguity in Bailey's 2006 *Titus*, where Lavinia's initial docile submission to suffocation by her father changed to spasms that may or may not have been an attempt to escape, but I have been unable to find any record of a Lavinia who retreated in horror as her father advanced on her, or who desperately struggled as he strangled or stabbed her, even though Saturninus' shocked reaction – "What hast thou done, unnatural and unkind?" (5.3.47) – arguably supports such a staging as much as if not more than it supports consensual euthanasia.[148] Moreover, some twenty

---

[146] Friedman and Dessen, *Titus*, pp. 99–104, 189. The production (dir. Gregory Doran, 1995) in which Lavinia resisted Titus's revenge on Chiron and Demetrius repeated certain music and dance motifs from the rape scene in her death scene, "complicat[ing] Titus's putative act of mercy by associating it with the brutal violation Lavinia had already endured."

[147] Friedman and Dessen, *Titus*, pp. 251–252.

[148] Whipday, "My tears," 259–260. The tradition of "euthanized" Lavinias, however, may finally be changing: in the winter of 2023, Jude Christian's all-female

years after Aebischer remarked on "the sheer endorsement Titus receives from critics and performers alike for his wresting of [Lavinia] into another myth which prescribes her destruction," even Billing's recent analysis of Lavinia's Ovidian intertexuality, which specifically faults directors for failing to accord it enough weight in performance, still approves this death as "her eventual corporal release from the torment of physical and emotional suffering."[149] Philomela does not die at her father's hands under a patriarchal rationale of shame. Why is it so unthinkable that Lavinia, once fully avenged in the mode of her choosing, might actually want to *live*?

To imagine Lavinia, mute and handless, still standing at the end of *Titus Andronicus* to weep over her father's corpse alongside her uncle, brother, and nephew, is not to imagine a happy ending, any more than it is to imagine *Women Beware Women*'s Bianca living on in the Florentine court as the safely wedded wife of her own rapist, forty years her senior. No revenge, however satisfying, erases the trauma of a violent physical attack; no amount of resigned pragmatism equates to the blissful self-determination of being with a man of one's own choosing. But these plays, in their divergence from the Lucrece paradigm, do show, however briefly, that life can go on, that a woman can live through rape without being so irrevocably polluted, and so shamed by that pollution, that her life can never again be worth living. To evoke disgust in a way that directs it where it belongs, toward the man who would force his body, its undesired and therefore utterly repulsive smells and tastes and fluids, onto a resisting woman, is not only to represent the crime from its victim's perspective, but to effect a subtle change in her condition: making the rapist the primary object of physical disgust shifts the victim's position from the gendered and

production of *Titus* at the Sam Wanamaker playhouse staged Lavinia's death as less than consensual. Each member of the cast carried a candle that represented her character's life and was snuffed out (often in some inventively violent way) upon that character's death. In the final scene, Lavinia walked around the table to meet her father, but tried to wrest her candle away from him when he seized it, frantically shaking her head with a look of shock as he blew it out. (Aebischer, personal communication, April 17, 2023; Kirwan, *Titus*.)

[149] Aebischer, "Silencing," 33; Billing, "Cutting Ovid's Tongue," 68.

permanent one of a woman defiled by nonmarital intercourse, to the ungendered and usually temporary one of an individual contaminated by involuntary contact with something revolting. To *be* a rotten orange, a piece of flyblown meat, a spider-infested cup of wine, a cistern crawling with toads, a pool of vomit, a latrine, a ditch full of sewage, or a vault of rotting carcasses is to inhabit a hopeless state of disgustingness; to be the unfortunate individual who has unwillingly come into contact with disgusting filth is to emerge contaminated, but eager for purification: a good bath; a socially respectable marriage; a really thoroughgoing revenge. Disgust, put to its proper uses, is capable of mitigating, or even erasing, shame.

Coda

For some readers, this Element will evoke the alterity of the past, a world still bound by pre-Christian pollution taboos, ancient medical concepts like *cacochymia*, and archaic laws. Others, however, will be all too familiar with the dictates of sexual purity and the ways disgust is deployed to police its boundaries. I want to end, then, by bringing the concerns of this study into the present, through a consideration of the (largely) American phenomenon that's become known as "purity culture": a movement most widespread within evangelical circles, but not confined to them, and most prominent in the 1990s and first decade of the 2000s, but still being repackaged for a new generation of adolescents today.[150] The central tenet of purity culture is that sexual activity – the definition of which can be extended to include kissing,

---

[150] My focus on American evangelical purity culture is not to ignore how ideologies of sexual purity operate in other cultures and religions worldwide, but to keep my critique more or less within the bounds of my own lived experience. Raised in an evangelical family, I escaped the excesses of purity culture mainly through the demographic luck of having been a teenager in the 1980s rather than the 1990s; being Canadian may also have been some protection, although Canadian evangelicals tend to take their cues from their American counterparts. It was perfectly clear, however, to a Canadian evangelical teenager in the 1980s that premarital sex was a special category of sin that could not be fully expunged by repentance.

hugging, sexual fantasies, masturbation, and pretty much anything else the zeal of its proponents might choose – must be wholly avoided until (heterosexual) marriage; failure to do so is not only sinful, but dooms one to psychological trauma, an inability to bond with one's eventual spouse, and a permanently unsatisfying marital sex life. While both males and females are supposed to live by these doctrines, women are, of course, expected to be the sexual gatekeepers, responsible for keeping the powerful male sexual urge in check by observing strict standards of "modesty" before marriage and submissively satisfying their husbands' sexual needs afterwards.[151] Purity culture, which explicitly upholds evangelical Christianity's valorization of traditional gender roles and the patriarchal domestic hierarchy, would have been damaging enough had it stayed within the religious tradition that spawned it. But evangelicals live to evangelize, and the American separation of church and state has always been tenuous: by the early 1990s, the beliefs of the purity movement had become the basis for US government-funded abstinence-only sex education.[152]

As the word itself indicates, the assumptions and practices of purity culture constitute the body that engages in nonmarital sexual activity as *impure* – polluted, contaminated, unclean – and, as in Shakespeare's England, that impure body is inevitably female. In a culture that places the responsibility for both sexes' abstinence squarely on the shoulders of young women, what better way to ensure women's compliance than by persuading them that sexual contact makes their bodies *disgusting*? One of the favored tactics of purity "educators" is to induce visceral disgust in their audiences and then link it rhetorically to the sexually polluted female body: the woman who is not a virgin on her wedding night is a piece of chewed gum, a used tissue, a sucked lollipop, a strip of tape rendered unsticky by the hair and dead skin from someone's arm. As seeing a disgusting thing is even more powerful than hearing about it, such

---

[151] Forrest, "Dispatches from Purity Culture."

[152] For a brief overview of how the American purity movement aligned with abstinence-only education, see Estrada, "Clinical Considerations"; on the failures of abstinence-only education and its continued influence despite them, see Boyer, "New Name."

lessons frequently involve elaborate theatrical demonstrations: progressive Christian blogger Joe Forrest recalls one such performance at his church youth group, where the speaker invited three teenage boys to spit with throat-clearing gusto into a pitcher of water. When a fourth boy – understandably – refused to drink it, the speaker informed the girls that "every time [they] have sex with a guy before marriage, it's like having someone spit in this water pitcher."[153] A colleague of mine, subjected in the 1990s to abstinence-only sex education at her Seattle public high school, watched a speaker brandish an expensive, new, still-wrapped toothbrush and then a cheap unwrapped one, its bristles battered, stained, and obviously used. Not quite the master of his metaphor, he addressed himself to the boys in the audience and asked them which toothbrush they'd rather use on their wedding night. The repugnance with which we regard others' sputum and saliva, as the chewed gum and sucked lollipop examples also suggest, would seem to make them an effectively disgusting stand-in for the defiling properties of semen.

In a system that so carefully and deliberately performs disgust for sexually "impure" women, the beliefs about sin, repentance, and having one's sin "washed away" that are putatively at the heart of evangelical Christianity are effectively derailed. Writing from a Christian perspective, Richard Beck observes the problems caused by his own religious tradition's use of contamination metaphors for a very small and mainly sexual subset of sins. Whereas most "minor" sins, such as telling a lie or succumbing to unjustified anger, are described with ambulatory metaphors – the sinner "stumbles," but can easily "get back on the straight and narrow path" – sexual sins "are often and uniquely characterized by contamination metaphors, and thus carry the psychological freight of disgust: loathing, strong aversion, visceral revulsion. Further... the *permanence property* of contamination – once contaminated, always contaminated – implies that 'contamination sins' are not so easily overcome. Contamination is not a 'mistake' where we can 'pick ourselves up' to 'try again.' Rather, once we appraise ourselves as

---

[153] Forrest, "Dispatches from Purity Culture." See also Valenti, *Purity Myth*, pp. 32–33, 41–42.

polluted the self-loathing is both intense and, potentially, permanent."[154] "A person begins life untouched," writes Samantha Field about her own experience within evangelical purity culture, "but the more one is touched, the more one is sullied. Not only does this make maintaining purity virtually impossible, it also creates the belief that this state is irreversible. Oh, God can forgive you, we're assured, but we can never *really* go back."[155]

In any religion where nonmarital sex is a special category of sin, governed not by the usual doctrinal structures of human guilt and divine forgiveness but by the far more inexorable laws of pollution and disgust, the crime of sexual assault places its victim in a position as untenable as that of Shakespeare's Lucrece. Quite aside from the responsibility that evangelical purity culture assigns to a woman for her own assault – any infraction of the rules of "modesty," or doing anything at all that might risk arousing a male, is an invitation to rape[156] – the assumption of irreversible contamination attaches itself to even those victims who by the very standards of purity culture cannot be deemed guilty of sin. The 2002 case of Elizabeth Smart, a fourteen-year-old Mormon girl abducted at knifepoint from her own bedroom, offers a powerful example of the harm caused by policing female sexuality through disgust. In interviews several years after her rescue, Smart spoke out against the abstinence-only sex education she'd received. Subjected daily to rape by her abductor, she felt "so dirty and so filthy" that for the nine months she was held captive, escape seemed not impossible but futile: "I thought, 'Oh my gosh, I'm that chewed up piece of gum, nobody re-chews a piece of gum. You throw it away.' And that's how easy it is to feel like you no longer have worth, you no longer have value. Why would it even be worth screaming out? Why would it even make a difference if you are rescued? Your life still has no value."[157] Smart's "educators," no doubt, would have hastened to assure her that the sin of sexual impurity lies wholly in the sinful desire and intent of the sinner, that *of course* an unwilling victim like herself is blameless. But, one might reply, if the sin of *consensual* premarital intercourse cannot

---

[154] Beck, "Spiritual Pollution," 59. [155] Field, "How We Teach Purity Culture."
[156] Ibid. [157] Frumin, "Elizabeth Smart."

be fully "washed away" by God's forgiveness – if sexual sin effects some irrevocable change in a woman that the non-contaminating sins do not – then it must be something about *the act itself*, and not the intentions behind the act, that renders the woman worthless.

To be raped is to be disgusted: the transgression of boundaries and contact with another's bodily fluids in sexual activity require physical attraction, erotic desire, sometimes even romantic love to transform them into pleasure. Without desire – when forced onto us by a person who is utterly *un*desired – they become the very definition of disgusting.[158] If the early modern theatre could occasionally, in plays like *Women Beware Women* and *Titus Andronicus*, offer a glimpse of how a woman might direct such disgust back at her rapist, what can be said about those who, four hundred years later, still promote beliefs that load moral and social stigma onto a survivor's sense of physical contamination?

They should be ashamed of themselves.

[158] Miller, *Anatomy*, pp. 137–138; Badour *et al.*, "Mental Contamination," 697–698.

Bibliography

Aebischer, Pascale. *Shakespeare's Violated Bodies: Stage and Screen Performance*. Cambridge University Press, 2004.

"Women Filming Rape in Shakespeare's *Titus Andronicus*: Jane Howell and Julie Taymore." *Études Anglaises* 55 (2002): 136–147.

"'Yet I'll Speak': Silencing the Female Voice in *Othello* and *Titus Andronicus*." *Actes de Congrès de la Société Française Shakespeare* 17 (1999): 27–46.

Ahmed, Sara. *The Cultural Politics of Emotion*. Routledge, 2004.

Allen, Peter Lewis. *The Wages of Sin: Sex and Disease, Past and Present*. University of Chicago Press, 2000.

Attridge, Derek. *The Work of Literature*. Oxford University Press, 2015.

Augustine. *The City of God*, translated by Marcus Dods. Modern Library, 2000.

Austin, John L. *How to Do Things with Words*. Harvard University Press, 1962.

Badour, Christal L., Matthew T. Feldner, Heidemarie Blumenthal, and Sarah J. Bujarski. "Examination of Increased Mental Contamination as a Potential Mechanism in the Association between Disgust Sensitivity and Sexual Assault-Related Posttraumatic Stress. *Cognitive Therapy and Research* 37 (2013): 697–703.

Baines, Barbara J. "Effacing Rape in Early Modern Representation." *ELH* 65 (1998): 69–89.

Bamford, Karen. *Sexual Violence on the Jacobean Stage*. Macmillan, 2000.

Barker, Roberta. "'A Freshly Creepy Reality': Jacobean Tragedy and Realist Acting on the Contemporary Stage." *Performing Early Modern Drama Today*, edited by Pascale Aebischer and Kathryn Prince. Cambridge University Press, 2012, pp. 121–141.

Basch, Michael Franz. "The Concept of Affect: A Re-Examination." *Journal of the American Psychoanalytic Association* 24 (1976): 759–778.

Beck, Richard. "Spiritual Pollution: The Dilemma of Sociomoral Disgust and the Ethic of Love." *Journal of Psychology and Theology* 34.1 (2006): 53–65.

Becon, Thomas. *The Governaunce of Vertue*. London, 1566. Early English Books Online. https://www.proquest.com/eebo/docview/2240935595/99837105/C1A06FEBBF9A4E80PQ/4?accountid=14701&sourcetype=Books

Belling, Catherine. "Infectious Rape, Therapeutic Revenge: Bloodletting and the Health of Rome's Body." *Disease, Diagnosis, and Cure on the Early Modern Stage*, edited by Stephanie Moss and Kaara L. Peterson. Ashgate, 2004, pp. 114–132.

Belsey, Catherine. "Tarquin Dispossessed: Expropriation and Consent in *The Rape of Lucrece*." *Shakespeare Quarterly* 52.3 (2001): 315–335.

Bernstein, Robin. "Toward the Integration of Theatre History and Affect Studies: Shame and the Rude Mechs' *The Method Gun*." *Theatre Journal* 64.2 (2012): 213–230.

Biggs, Murray. "Does the Duke Rape Bianca in Middleton's *Women Beware Women*?" *Notes and Queries* 44.1 (1997): 97–100.

Billing, Christian M. "'Though This be Method, Yet There is Madness In't': Cutting Ovid's Tongue in Recent Stage and Film Performances of *Titus Andronicus*." *Shakespeare Survey* 69 (2016): 58–78.

Boeckl, Christine M. *Images of Leprosy: Disease, Religion, and Politics in European Art*. Truman State University Press, 2011.

Boyer, Jesseca. "New Name, Same Harm: Rebranding of Federal Abstinence-Only Programs." *Guttmacher Institute*, February 28, 2018. www.guttmacher.org/gpr/2018/02/new-name-same-harm-rebranding-federal-abstinence-only-programs.

Brathwaite, Richard. *The English Gentlewoman*. London, 1631. Early English Books Online. https://www.proquest.com/eebo/docview/2240907400/A10D8C3CF71B4FC8PQ/1?accountid=14701&sourcetype=Books&imgSeq=1

Brockman, Sonya L. "Trauma and Abandoned Testimony in *Titus Andronicus* and *Rape of Lucrece*." *College Literature* 44.3 (2017): 344–378.

Bromham, A. A. "A Plague Will Come: Art, Rape, and Venereal Disease in Middleton's *Women Beware Women*." *EnterText* 3.1 (2003): 45–60.

Bromley, Laura. "Lucrece's Re-Creation." *Shakespeare Quarterly* 34 (1983): 200–211.

Brottman, Mikita. *Offensive Films: Toward an Anthropology of Cinéma Vomitif*. Vanderbilt University Press, 2005.

Brown, Georgia. "Afterword." *Disgust in Early Modern English Literature*, edited by Natalie K. Eschenbaum and Barbara Correll. Routledge, 2016, pp. 201–212.

Brown, Karin. "Professional Productions of Early Modern Drama in the UK and USA, 1960–2010." *Performing Early Modern Drama Today*, edited by Pascale Aebischer and Kathryn Prince. Cambridge University Press, 2012, pp. 178–217.

Burrus, Virginia. *Saving Shame: Martyrs, Saints, and Other Abject Subjects*. University of Pennsylvania Press, 2008.

Catty, Jocelyn. *Writing Rape, Writing Women in Early Modern England*. Macmillan, 1999.

Connolly, Annaliese. "In the Repertoire." *Women Beware Women: A Critical Guide*, edited by Andrew Hiscock. Continuum, 2011, pp. 59–76.

Daalder, Joost. "The State of the Art." *Women Beware Women: A Critical Guide*, edited by Andrew Hiscock. Continuum, 2011, pp. 77–96.

Daileader, Celia R. "Writing Rape, Raping Rites: Shakespeare's and Middleton's Lucrece Poems." *Violence, Politics, and Gender in Early Modern England*, edited by Joseph P. Ward. Palgrave, 2008, pp. 67–89.

Dawson, Anthony B. "Women Beware Women and the Economy of Rape." *Studies in English Literature 1500–1900* 27.2 (1987): 303–320.

Detmer-Goebel, Emily. "The Need for Lavinia's Voice: *Titus Andronicus* and the Telling of Rape." *Shakespeare Studies* 29 (2001): 75–92.

  "'What More Could Woman Do?' Dramatizing Consent in Heywood's *Rape of Lucrece* and Middleton's *Woman Beware Women*." *Women's Studies* 36 (2007): 141–159.

Dickson, Andrew. "The Gory Details of *Titus Andronicus*: 'Blood Gets Everywhere, Actors Slip on it.'" *The Guardian*, February 8, 2016. www.theguardian.com/stage/2016/feb/08/titus-andronicus-rsc-blood-actors.

Dixon, Thomas. "Violence, Vomit, and Hysteria: An Interview with Rose Reynolds." *The History of Emotions Blog*, October 3, 2013. https://emotionsblog.history.qmul.ac.uk/2013/10/violence-vomit-and-hysteria-an-interview-with-rose-reynolds/.

Dolan, Frances. "Re-reading Rape in *The Changeling*." *Journal for Early Modern Cultural Studies* 11.1 (2011): 4–29.

Donaldson, Ian. *The Rapes of Lucretia: A Myth and Its Transformations*. Clarendon, 1982.

Douglas, Mary. *Purity and Danger: An Analysis of Concepts of Pollution and Taboo*. 1966, rpt. Routledge, 1995.

Dubrow, Heather. *Captive Victors: Shakespeare's Narrative Poems and Sonnets*. Cornell University Press, 1987.

Eschenbaum, Natalie K. "Desiring Disgust in Robert Herrick's Epigrams." *Disgust in Early Modern English Literature*, edited by Natalie K. Eschenbaum and Barbara Correll. Routledge, 2016, pp. 53–68.

Eschenbaum, Natalie K., and Barbara Correll. "Introduction." *Disgust in Early Modern English Literature*, edited by Natalie K. Eschenbaum and Barbara Correll. Routledge, 2016, pp. 1–19.

Estrada, Lauren Leigh. "Clinical Considerations of the Evangelical Purity Movement's Impact on Female Sexuality. *Journal of Sex and Marital Therapy* 48.2 (2022): 121–132.

Field, Samantha. "How We Teach Purity Culture Isn't the Problem – Purity Culture Itself Is the Problem." *Rewire News Group*, October 24, 2016. https://rewirenewsgroup.com/2016/10/24/teach-purity-culture-isnt-problem-purity-culture-problem/.

Fineman, Joel. "Shakespeare's Will: The Temporality of Rape." *Representations* 20 (1980): 25–76.

Fitzherbert, John. *Here Begynneth a Newe Tracte or Treatyse Moost P[ro]fytable for all Husba[n]de Men*. London, 1530. Early English Books Online. https://www.proquest.com/eebo/docview/2240932425/99847507/72B948B5450C4EE9PQ/4?accountid=14701&sourcetype=Books

Fletcher, John. "The Tragedy of Valentinian." *Four Jacobean Sex Tragedies*, edited by Martin Wiggins. Oxford University Press, 1998, pp. 233–328.

Forey, Madeleine, ed. *Ovid's Metamorphoses*, translated by Arthur Golding. Johns Hopkins University Press, 2001.

Forrest, Joe. "Dispatches from Purity Culture: How Sexual Shame Overtook a Generation." *Instrument of Mercy*, August 1, 2018. https://instrumentofmercy.com/2018/08/01/dispatches-from-purity-culture/.

Foster, Verna Ann. "The Deed's Creature: The Tragedy of Bianca in *Women Beware Women*." *Journal of English and Germanic Philology* 78 (1979): 508–521.

Friedman, Michael D., and Alan Dessen. *Titus Andronicus*. 2nd ed. Shakespeare in Performance Series. Manchester University Press, 2013.

Frumin, Aliyah. "Elizabeth Smart: Abstinence-Only Education Can Make Rape Survivors Feel 'Dirty,' 'Filthy'." *NBC News*, May 6, 2013. www.nbcnews.com/id/wbna51793513#.XaXnA5NKi88.

Gill, Roma, ed. *Women Beware Women*, by Thomas Middleton. Benn, 1968.

Goldstein, David. *Eating and Ethics in Shakespeare's England*. Cambridge University Press, 2013.

Gossett, Suzanne. "'Best Men are Molded out of Faults': Marrying the Rapist in Jacobean Drama." *English Literary Renaissance* 14.3 (1984): 305–327.

Greenstadt, Amy. *Rape and the Rise of the Author*. Ashgate, 2001.

Gyer, Nicholas. *The English Phlebotomy*. London, 1592. Early English Books Online. https://www.proquest.com/eebo/docview/2240873171/99847507/E613DD4B600D47FBPQ/1?accountid=14701&sourcetype=Books

Hagthorpe, John. *Divine Meditations, and Elegies*. London, 1622. Early English Books Online. https://www.proquest.com/eebo/docview/2248586661/99847507/CD8A84906EC14DCFPQ/1?accountid=14701&sourcetype=Books

Hall, Joseph. "Noah's Dove." *The Works of Joseph Hall B. of Exceter*. London, 1634, pp. 507–521. Early English Books Online. https://www.proquest.com/eebo/docview/2248499188/A5AC45259DA04313PQ/8?accountid=14701&sourcetype=Books&imgSeq=1

Hall, Michael. "'Lewd but Familiar Eyes': The Narrative Tradition of Rape and Shakespeare's *The Rape of Lucrece*." *Women, Violence, and English Renaissance Literature: Essays Honoring Paul Jorgensen*, edited by Linda Woodbridge and Sharon Beehler. Arizona Center for Medieval and Renaissance Studies, 2003, pp. 51–71.

Harward, Simon. *Harward's Phlebotomy*. London, 1601. Early English Books Online. https://www.proquest.com/eebo/docview/2240873249/99847507/CE6B8A9ADB964D4DPQ/1?accountid=14701&sourcetype=Books

Heller, Jennifer L. "Space, Violence and Bodies in Middleton and Cary." *Studies in English Literature 1500–1900* 45.2 (2005): 425–441.

Herz, Rachel. *That's Disgusting: Unraveling the Mysteries of Repulsion.* Norton, 2012.

Hobgood, Allison P. *Passionate Playgoing in Early Modern England.* Cambridge University Press, 2014.

Hotz-Davies, Ingrid. "A Chaste Maid in Cheapside and Women Beware Women: Feminism, Anti-Feminism, and the Limitations of Satire." *Cahiers Elisabethains* 39 (1991): 29–39.

Houen, Alex. "Introduction: Affecting Words." *Textual Practice* 25.2 (2011): 215–232.

Howard, Jean E. "Interrupting the Lucrece Effect? The Performance of Rape on the Early Modern Stage." *The Oxford Handbook of Shakespeare and Embodiment: Gender, Sexuality, and Race*, edited by Valerie Traub. Oxford University Press, 2016, pp. 657–672.

Hurley, Erin. *Theatre and Feeling.* Palgrave, 2010.

Hutchings, Mark. "Middleton's *Women Beware Women*: Rape, Seduction, or Power, Simply?" *Notes and Queries* 45.3 (1998): 366–367.

Jed, Stephanie H. *Chaste Thinking: The Rape of Lucretia and the Birth of Humanism.* Indiana University Press, 1989.

Kahn, Coppélia. "New Directions: 'Two Kings in One Throne': Lust, Love, and Marriage in *Women Beware Women*." *Women Beware Women: A Critical Guide*, edited by Andrew Hiscock. Continuum, 2011, pp. 156–170.

"The Rape in Shakespeare's *Lucrece*." *Shakespeare Studies* 9 (1976): 45–72.

Roman Shakespeare: Warriors, Wounds, and Women. Routledge, 1997.

Kelly, Daniel. *Yuck!: The Nature and Moral Significance of Disgust.* MIT Press, 2011.

Kenny, Amy. "A 'Dummy Corpse Full of Bones and Entrails': Staging Dismemberment in the Early Modern Playhouse." *Humorality in Early Modern Art, Material Culture, and Performance*, edited by Amy Kenny and Kaara L. Peterson. Palgrave, 2021, pp. 85–101.

Kirwan, Peter. "*Titus Andronicus* (Shakespeare's Globe) @ The Sam Wanamaker Playhouse." *The Bardathon*, March 12, 2023. https://drpeterkirwan.com/2023/03/12/titus-andronicus-shakespeares-globe-the-sam-wanamaker-playhouse/.

Kolnai, Aurel. *Disgust*, translated by Elizabeth Kolnai and Barry Smith. Open Court, 2004.

Korsmeyer, Carolyn. *Savouring Disgust: The Foul and the Fair in Aesthetics*. Oxford University Press, 2011.

Kupfer, Tom R. "Why Are Injuries Disgusting? Comparing Pathogen Avoidance and Empathy Accounts." *Emotion* 18.7 (2018): 959–970.

Lechler, Kate. "Thomas Middleton in Performance 1960–2013: A History of Reception," unpublished Ph.D. thesis, Florida State University, 2014, p. 55.

Lemnius, Levinus. *The Touchstone of Complexions*. London, 1576.

Levin, Richard A. "If Women Should Beware Women, Bianca Should Beware Mother." *Studies in English Literature 1500–1900* 37.2 (1997): 371–389.

Little, Arthur L. Jr. *Shakespeare Jungle Fever: National-Imperial Re-Visions of Race, Rape, and Sacrifice*. Stanford University Press, 2001.

MacGregor, Catherine. "Undoing the Body Politic: Representing Rape in *Women Beware Women*." *Theatre Research International* 23.1 (1998): 14–23.

Markham, Gervase. *Countrey Contentments, or The English Huswife*. London, 1623. Early English Books Online. https://www.proquest.com/eebo/docview/2240948141/99847507/9D002A6CBA9942BAPQ/4?accountid=14701&sourcetype=Books

   Markham's Farwell to Husbandry. London, 1620. Early English Books Online. https://www.proquest.com/eebo/docview/2240937350/99847507/4015E5203E0C440EPQ/4?accountid=14701&sourcetype=Books

Marshall, Cynthia. *The Shattering of the Self: Violence, Subjectivity, and Early Modern Texts*. Johns Hopkins University Press, 2002.

Marston, John. *The Dutch Courtesan*, edited by David Crane. A & C Black, 1997.

Martin, Christopher. *Constituting Old Age in Early Modern English Literature from Queen Elizabeth to King Lear*. University of Massachusetts Press, 2012.

Maus, Katharine Eisaman. "Taking Tropes Seriously: Language and Violence in Shakespeare's *Rape of Lucrece*." *Shakespeare Quarterly* 37.1 (1986): 66–82.

McConachie, Bruce. *Engaging Audiences: A Cognitive Approach to Spectating in the Theatre*. Palgrave, 2008.

McGinn, Colin. *The Meaning of Disgust*. Oxford University Press, 2011.

Menninghaus, Winfried. *Disgust: Theory and History of a Strong Sensation*, translated by Howard Eiland and Joel Golb. State University of New York Press, 2003.

Mentz, Steven. "*Women Beware Women*, and: *The Winter's Tale*, and: *The Merchant of Venice* (review)." *Shakespeare Bulletin* 27.4 (2009): 669–681.

Middleton, Thomas. *Thomas Middleton: The Collected Works*, edited by Gary Taylor and John Lavagnino. Oxford University Press, 2007.

Miller, William Ian. *The Anatomy of Disgust*. Harvard University Press, 1997.

Mills, Geoff. "Review: *Titus Andronicus* at the Royal Shakespeare Theatre." *Exeunt*, July 17, 2017. http://exeuntmagazine.com/reviews/titus-andronicus-blanche-mcintyre/.

Moses, Diana C. "Livy's Lucretia and the Validity of Coerced Consent in Roman Law." *Consent and Coercion to Sex and Marriage in Ancient and Medieval Societies*, edited by Angeliki E. Laiou. Dunbarton Oaks Research Library and Collection, 1993, pp. 39–81.

Mullaney, Steven. *The Reformation of Emotions in the Age of Shakespeare*. University of Chicago Press, 2015.

Newman, Jane O. "'And Let Mild Women to Him Lose Their Mildness': Philomela, Female Violence, and Shakespeare's *The Rape of Lucrece*." *Shakespeare Quarterly* 45.3 (1994): 304–326.

Noble, Louise. *Medical Cannibalism in Early Modern Literature and Culture*. Palgrave, 2011.

Oldham, Thomas A. "The Affective Appeal of Violence and the Violent Appeal of Affect: *Titus Andronicus*, Lucy Bailey, and Shakespeare's Globe." *Shakespeare Bulletin* 40.1 (2022): 69–88.

Packard, Bethany. "Lavinia as Coauthor of Shakespeare's *Titus Andronicus*." *Studies in English Literature 1500–1900* 50.2 (2010): 281–300.

Panek, Jennifer. "Bad Dancing and Contagious Embarrassment in *More Dissemblers besides Women*." *Contagion and the Shakespearean Stage*, edited by Mary Floyd-Wilson and Darryl Chalk. Palgrave, 2019, pp. 147–168.

  "Shame and Pleasure in *The Changeling*." *Renaissance Drama* 42.2 (2014): 191–215.

  "*The Nice Valour*'s Anatomy of Shame." *English Literary Renaissance* 48.3 (2018): 339–367.

  "This Base Stallion Trade': He-Whores and Male Sexuality on the Early Modern Stage." *English Literary Renaissance* 40.3 (2010): 357–392.

Paster, Gail Kern. *The Body Embarrassed: Drama and the Disciplines of Shame in Early Modern England*. Cornell University Press, 1993.

Pechter, Edward. *Othello and Interpretive Traditions*. University of Iowa Press, 1999.

Reynoldes, Edward. *A Treatise of the Passions and Faculties of the Soule of Man*. London, 1640. Early English Books Online. https://www.proquest.com/eebo/docview/2240857245/99847507/1BF1A58B75E84FF8PQ/7?accountid=14701&sourcetype=Books

Roach, Joseph. *The Player's Passion: Studies in the Science of Acting*. University of Delaware Press, 1985.

Roberts, Sasha. *Reading Shakespeare's Poems in Early Modern England*. Palgrave, 2003.

Robertson, Karen. "Rape and the Appropriation of Progne's Revenge in Shakespeare's *Titus Andronicus*, or 'Who Cooks the Thyestean Banquet'?" *Representing Rape in Medieval and Early Modern Literature*, edited by Elizabeth Robertson and Christine M. Rose. Palgrave, 2001, pp. 214–237.

Robinson, Benedict. "Disgust c. 1600." *ELH* 81.2 (2014): 553–583.

Rozin, Paul, and April E. Fallon. "A Perspective on Disgust." *Psychological Review* 94.1 (1987): 23–41.

Rozin, Paul, Jonathan Haidt, and Clark McCauley. "Disgust." *Handbook of Emotions*, edited by Lisa Feldman Barrett, Michael Lewis, and Jeanette M. Haviland-Jones. Guilford, 2016, pp. 816–836.

Sale, Carolyn. "Representing Lavinia: The (In)significance of Women's Consent in Legal Discourses of Rape and Ravishment and Shakespeare's *Titus Andronicus*." *Women, Violence, and English Renaissance Literature: Essays Honoring Paul Jorgensen*, edited by Linda Woodbridge and Sharon Beehler. Arizona Center for Medieval and Renaissance Studies, 2003, pp. 1–27.

Sanchez, Melissa. *Erotic Subjects: The Sexuality of Politics in Early Modern English Literature*. Oxford University Press, 2011.

Shakespeare, William. *The Norton Shakespeare*, edited by Stephen Greenblatt, Walter Cohen, Jean E. Howard, and Katharine Eisaman Maus. 2nd ed. Norton, 2008.

　The Winter's Tale, edited by John Pitcher. Methuen, 2010.

　The Rape of Lucrece. *The Poems*, edited by John Roe. Cambridge University Press, 2006, pp. 147–238.

Siena, Kevin. "The Clean and the Foul: Paupers and the Pox in London Hospitals, c. 1500-c. 1700." *Sins of the Flesh: Responding to Sexual Disease in Early Modern Europe*, edited by Kevin Siena. Centre for Reformation and Renaissance Studies, 2005, pp. 261–284.

Smith, Peter J. "Exonerating Rape: Pornography as Exculpation in Shakespeare's *The Rape of Lucrece*." *Shakespeare* 5.4 (2009): 407–422. "*Women Beware Women*." *Cahiers Elizabethains* 36 (1989): 90–91.

Solga, Kim. *Violence against Women in Early Modern Performance*. Palgrave, 2009.

Steggle, Matthew. *Laughing and Weeping in Early Modern Theatres*. Ashgate, 2007.

Taylor, Gary. "Gender, Hunger, Horror: The History and Significance of *The Bloody Banquet*." *Journal of Early Modern Cultural Studies* 1.1 (2001): 1–45.

Tempera, Mariangela. "*Titus Andronicus*: Staging the Mutilated Roman Body." *Questioning Bodies in Shakespeare's Rome*, edited by Maria Del Sapio Garbero, Nancy Isenberg, and Maddalena Pennacchia. V&R Unipress, 2010, pp. 109–119.

Tilmouth, Christopher. "Shakespeare's Open Consciences." *Renaissance Studies* 23 (2009): 501–515.

Toulalan, Sarah. *Imagining Sex: Pornography and Bodies in Seventeenth-Century England*. Oxford University Press, 2007.

Tribble, Evelyn. "Affective Contagion on the Early Modern Stage." *Affect Theory and Early Modern Texts: Politics, Ecology, and Form*, edited by Amanda Bailey and Mario Di Gangi. Palgrave, 2017, pp. 195–212.

Valenti, Jessica. *The Purity Myth: How America's Obsession with Virginity Is Hurting Young Women*. Seal Press, 2009.

Vertue, Henry. *A Plea for Peace: or, A Sermon Preached in St. Paul's Church in London July 9, 1637*. London, 1637.

Walker, Garthine. "Rereading Rape and Sexual Violence in Early Modern England." *Gender and History* 10.1 (1998): 1–25.

Wentersdorf, Kyle P. "Animal Symbolism in Shakespeare's *Hamlet*: The Imagery of Sex Nausea." *Comparative Drama* 17.4 (1983): 348–382.

Whipday, Emma. "'My Tears Will Choke Me If I ope my mouth': Framing, Feasting, and Speaking Sexual Violence in *Titus Andronicus*, 2006–2017." *Titus Andronicus: The State of Play*, edited by Farah Karim-Cooper. Bloomsbury, 2019, pp. 249–270.

Williams, Caroline D. "'Silence Like a Lucrece Knife': Shakespeare and the Meanings of Rape." *Yearbook of English Studies* 23 (1993): 93–110.

Willis, Deborah. "'The Gnawing Vulture': Revenge, Trauma Theory, and *Titus Andronicus*." *Shakespeare Quarterly* 53 (2002): 21–52.

Cambridge Elements $\equiv$

Shakespeare Performance

W. B. Worthen
Barnard College

W. B. Worthen is Alice Brady Pels Professor in the Arts, and
Chair of the Theatre Department at Barnard College. He is also
co-chair of the Ph.D. Program in Theatre at Columbia University,
where he is Professor of English and Comparative Literature.

ABOUT THE SERIES

Shakespeare Performance is a dynamic collection in a field that is both always emerging and always evanescent. Responding to the global range of Shakespeare performance today, the series launches provocative, urgent criticism for researchers, graduate students and practitioners. Publishing scholarship with a direct bearing on the contemporary contexts of Shakespeare performance, it considers specific performances, material and social practices, ideological and cultural frameworks, emerging and significant artists, and performance histories.

Cambridge Elements ☰

Shakespeare Performance

Sleep No More and the Discourses of Shakespeare Performance
D. J. Hopkins

Extended Reality Shakespeare
Aneta Mancewicz

*Staging Disgust: Rape, Shame, and Performance in Shakespeare
and Middleton*
Jennifer Panek

A full series listing is available at: www.cambridge.org/ESPF

Printed in the United States
by Baker & Taylor Publisher Services